Flip It

How to buy, renovate and sell property with confidence

Karen Whatley & Tasha Darrington

Order this book online at www.tashaandkaren.com or on Amazon

A catalogue record for this book is available from the British Library: ISBN 978-1-9164543-0-9

Printed in Peterborough, Cambridgeshire, UK

ISBN: 978-1-9164543-0-9

www.tashaandkaren.com

For everyone who wants to have the confidence to start something new, build upon what they already have and create the life they deserve.

Contents

Section 4: How to minimise risk and maximise potential

Section 5: How to project manage with confidence

Section 1: Introduction

Section 1: Introduction

Prologue

About the authors - Tasha Darrington

So, how did I get into property and flipping? I can remember from an early age always wanting something different, never knowing what that was, and being guided by my teachers or peers as to which way to go. School was ok, but all I wanted to do was get out into the world, earn some money, have fun and enjoy life. When Karen and I did some personal development work a few years ago looking at our values and what is important to us, I thought back to the early days and remembered back then, as it is now, that one of the most important values to me was to have fun. Not reckless fun, but the type of outdoorsy, carefree, spiritual kind of fun. But it felt wrong to say that; it felt selfish.

The truth is though, if you are doing what *you* want and living to *your* highest values, then you can influence the people around you in a positive way, which makes you feel less selfish when you have a different outlook on life. By being the best possible version of you, you can really help other people at the same time, but without feeling like you have to be the same as them.

I was young for my school year, so I did my GCSEs and left school early at 15 years of age. I had no idea what I wanted to do, so just applied for any jobs going. I got my first job straight away as an accounts clerk and was earning the amazing sum of £2.01 per hour (the minimum wage back then!)

I was excited to be out in the world and away from the restrictions of school.

The job was far from exciting. It was in an office, it was paperwork based, but I felt I had freedom and some cash too. I really wanted to learn to drive and get out into the world, although I never really knew where, but had to wait another 18 months for that.

I was made redundant from that job after about a year and went on to be 'lucky' enough to be made redundant another 3 times. For most people, being made redundant or the threat of potential redundancies in their workplace is really frightening. You feel rejected and uncertain of what to do next. Over the years, I have learned that you need to get uncomfortable in order to grow. Not many people realise this (well, you do now!) and looking back I ask myself '*what was I thinking*?' but you don't know what you don't know and you can easily get stuck in life.

I spent the next several years working for a range of companies in a variety of jobs that were not satisfying to say the least. I worked in office jobs and even as a white-van driver! One of the more exciting jobs was to work as a contractor for an IT company to try and 'save the world' from the millennium bug as 1 January 2000 was looming. Suffice to say that it came and went and we all made good money selling our services to 'fix' the problem, but once again I found myself looking for another job.

I really enjoyed the IT world, so got a job working for a company in Cambridge in their IT team. That lasted a couple of years, then I moved to a larger IT company in 2003. The new job upped my pay significantly and gave me the confidence to progress within the role. I doubled my salary within 5 years, just by asking for more each year.

The very first property I purchased was in 1998 for £65k. It was my first home and a very exciting time. I didn't know anything about property back then. In fact, the property was on the market for £70,000 and after viewing it and wanting to buy it, I went to see my mortgage advisor at the time who said I could afford up to £65,000.

Not knowing anything about the property market, when the estate agent called to see if I had liked the property I said "Yes", but that "I couldn't have it as I was only allowed to have a mortgage to buy a £65,000 property!"

I had no idea that you could 'offer' on properties, and the price it's on the market for doesn't really mean that's the price you pay. Oh how times have changed!

I bought my second residential property in 2004 for £245k. I was able to do this because I'd been asking for, and getting, a pay rise every year. I had also benefitted from a rising market. The property I had bought in 1998 for £65k was now worth £165k. This was with no effort from me – I just lived there. This was my first property lightbulb moment.

I met my partner and soul mate, Karen, in early 2005. She turned up one very cold and dark winter's evening to join our hockey team. In that same year we decided to 'have a little go' at property.

We had no idea where that decision would take us. There was no big vision. We just wanted to create some more income to give us more choice, which ultimately meant more fun.

The first property was so exciting. Even though we were both working full-time with long hours, we fully committed to working evenings and weekends to get the property renovated.

This truly was learning as you go, or by "*trial and (t)error*" as Karen would say, and it was exciting! We didn't have a plan, we didn't have any contacts of tradespeople, we had no idea where to buy materials, we had never done this before; but we had plenty of motivation, enthusiasm and were enjoying the process. The rest, as they say, is history…or at least in our case, now in a book!

This book has been written using all of the knowledge and experience we have gained over the past decade of flipping. If you are just beginning and are frightened, the best thing to do is to start.

Just go for it. With this book we will let you know what we did and we will share our failures and our triumphs. Take these and use them all to launch you to your goals. It's going to be *flipping* awesome!

About the authors - Karen Whatley

I grew up in a village in Hertfordshire with Mum, Dad and my younger brother. I worked hard at school, played hard at sports and worked a variety of part-time jobs alongside my education, before going to University. I wanted to do Criminology, my parents wanted me to get a business degree, so we compromised, and I found a University that offered a dual honours degree. My course was BA (Hons) Management and Criminology which might lead you to think that I have a degree in managing criminals, but actually they were two separate subjects with no cross-over. Anyway, it made it more interesting. Why do one subject when you can do two! As the saying goes, 'Women are great multi-taskers'!

I've always liked having my own money and I've never shied away from working really hard to get it. So for over 10 years now Tasha and I have been mastering the ins and outs of the property world together. My property journey started when I was 19 and bought my first home whilst at University. When I graduated I sold the property.

I moved to a different city for my first (and last) full time job, and I seemingly then took a sabbatical where I completely forgot about the potential that property could give me and instead focussed my attention on making my new bosses like me. At least that's what I thought I was doing. All I was really doing was working towards someone else's dream…. making the results happen that were required of me. I quickly realised that in the public sector there are two types of people; the ones who want to fit in and make a difference, and the ones who realise that they don't fit in but want to make a difference, which makes them stick out like a sore thumb, and inevitably makes change happen, either through innovation, disruption or getting themselves noticed and promoted. That was me.

Very early on in my career, the abridged version of what I was told was that "I probably wasn't right for local government…." It really hurt at the time because all I wanted was acceptance and praise from my (then) boss. I came to realise later that what she really meant and what I had interpreted in my naivety were two very different things.

Interesting, isn't it, that sometimes in life you need to go through a bit of pain in order to make a change. I guess that's why you bought this book; to make a change and learn a new skill that could provide chunky cash so that you can fix something or maybe improve something in your life.

In that moment when she said those words, I felt for the first time in my life, the only time in my life, that I was different. And I'm not. I have the same aspirations as everyone else, the same rights, the same dreams, the same pains, the same fears and the same joys. But one thing I will not stand for anymore is leaving myself open to that kind of exposure. I suddenly thought that if she didn't like me, then she could damage my good reputation. I also had the fleeting thought that I might not get another job because of her influence, which could mean no career progression, no income, and losing the life that I had built for myself.

Irrational as it now seems, it actually served as an awakening. It told me that I needed to get multiple income streams so that I could never be vulnerable again. It also told me that I needed to get out of that environment as soon as possible.

So I did. I applied for a promotion into another department and got it. Moving into the housing department gave me the knowledge and qualifications needed to stand me in brilliant stead to become a good landlord – one that plays by the rules, looks after their tenants and understands the value in going the extra mile to minimise voids and keep a happy household. It was also at that time that I met Tasha and we decided to buy our first house to refurbish. Meeting her and my new hockey team had a massive impact on restoring my self-worth and helping me deal with being in the same workplace as the person who had tormented me.

I stayed with that employer for a further few years and spent my final couple of years working as a project manager before leaving in 2011. See; local government was the right place for '*someone like me*'.

So why choose property when there are so many different asset classes you can select from? Well, for me it is the accessibility of it. I like it that the properties we renovate are physical commodities.

That means that as long as we buy locally, the number of variables is significantly reduced. I can drive by whenever I like to check that the tradespeople are on target. I can call in unannounced and be sure that work is progressing. We've never had an occasion where we've been taken for a ride, and I like having that confidence and knowledge.

It's a control thing I guess. As I get older I'm sure we'll diversify and invest into what I perceive to be less controllable cash generators than property such as stocks, shares, investing in other businesses, watches, classic cars, wine etc. But for now, we're focussed on property and will continue to be for the rest of our lives. It makes sense.

People often say to us, “Oh, I can’t flip property, that’s for builders”.

It’s not – many builders don’t flip for themselves either. They work on jobs for other people and are focussed on providing a service, going from one job to the next rather than flipping their own properties in order to invest the cash in an asset base, such as buy-to-lets as we have done. Either that, or they invest it in building themselves a spectacular home and then cash that in later in life and downsize or retire to the sunnier climates.

Anyone *can* flip property and make a profit, especially in a rising market. The difference between someone who does it once and was lucky because of the rising market, and those of us who make a proper business out of it, comes down to systems and processes. You never really know when you do your first or second flip whether it was fortune, fluke or by design.

By doing more and more flips, you start to see the trends in the market, the types of property that de-risk it best and the pitfalls. Over time the results you get will give you a good average. Some might not sell straight away. Some might sell and then the purchaser can’t get a mortgage and then you have to market it again, which costs you more, but makes it still viable overall. And some might make you more profit than you originally thought because the market has risen while you've owned it. Once you learn to accept that there will be upsides and downsides, you are on your way to building a successful business.

A good average is to predict that for every three flips you do, one will make the profit you expect, one will make a bit less than you predict (because the sale might fall out of bed the first time which costs you a bit more on the lending, council tax, utilities and red wine drowning your sorrows on the day you get that call) and one might make a bit more profit.

Accept this and move on, but systemise your business to take away the guesswork.

Introduction

This book has been written for anyone who wants to understand how to buy, renovate and sell residential property in the UK for profit.

Whether you are completely new to the concept of 'flipping', or a seasoned property investor; this book will help you because, unlike other property books, it focuses specifically on the niche of Buy to Sell.

"Wide diversification is only required when investors

do not understand what they are doing."

Warren Buffett

This is not a property management book or a renovation guide. It's a journey into the reality of property refurbishments and renovations, with real-life stories and examples throughout. Some of the names and locations have been changed to spare the embarrassment of some people… and some haven't!

Every Flip (property deal) and every Flipper (property developer) is different. But the foundations which underpin how to maximise the profit in every deal remain the same:

1. Buy for 'market value', or less
2. Add value or complete the refurbishment to the highest standard it warrants, given the relative cost and profit potential
3. Sell it for the best price achievable (but don't be greedy!)
4. Don't pay any more tax than you have to

Now, this is an over simplified list of actions and you may be thinking, '*well anyone can do that*' and quite honestly, you'd be right. The truth is anyone can; the reality is most people don't.

The majority of people in the world stick to one income stream – usually a job – and don't give property a second thought. Others will have a go at property and do the best job they can with the knowledge they have. If it doesn't work, they'll probably stop at flipping just one property but talk about it forever; putting off everyone around them with the pitfalls and doom and gloom stories of how they fell off a ladder or got ripped off by a plumber. Remember, this is their reality, not yours.

Your third type of person is the one that quietly gets on with it, picking up tips and hints but making mistakes along the way, earning an average living but never really turning it into a scalable business.

And then there are the '*Flip It*' Flippers. These are the people who will stop at nothing to make their dream of freedom, choice, leverage, systems, assets and a fulfilling life a reality. Once you have those things you can truly say that you are an experienced developer. These people often come to us for mentoring to help them take their business to the next level much faster.

When all is said and done, experienced developers will tell you that the way to succeed in this business is to *'fail forward fast'*. By that, we don't mean 'bodge it'. If you are going to make mistakes, and you will when you're learning anything new, then it'll happen with your cost estimations, management of trades or getting to market quickly. Make as many errors as you need to, but make them quickly, fix them, learn the lesson and move on. In the end, the most successful Flippers are the ones who get fewer things wrong than they get right, refining as they go along until they have a well drilled business.

Flip It is designed to help you avoid the mistakes that we, along with many others, have made and to show you how to systemise the whole process as quickly as you can in order to get started; turning your hobby into a business, or your business into an empire.

If you want another generic property investing book, then there are lots of them on Amazon. This isn't a book that will just give you a brief overview of everything in the world of property development.

What is unique about this book is that we give you an honest overview of flipping with resources you can access and tips you can implement right away. By the end of this book, you'll be ready to go out there and find your own flips.

In order to fully understand the opportunity that buying and selling property offers, it is important to understand that there are certain trends that will affect the property market. Let's begin by taking a brief look at the history of property ownership so that we fully understand what has happened and what might happen in the future.

This section will also help you see off the pessimists who will undoubtedly take an interest in what you're doing when you start to flip property and may try to dissuade you from continuing.

Remember, they are only doing it to protect you based on their own reality and experience.

Everyone *can* make money from flipping property, including you.

Section 2: Understanding the market and planning your future

Section 2 – Understanding the market and planning your future

Market forces

Looking back at property ownership in the UK through the 1900s and into the 21st century, there are some very interesting facts which help us to establish the ongoing need for Flippers. It gives us confidence that the Buy to Sell strategy is a sustainable business and definitely something worth investing time and effort into mastering.

In 1918, only 20% of properties were privately owned and by 1951 this percentage had risen to 29%. At the same time, the Conservatives came into power and by the time they were voted out in 1964, homeownership had risen to 45%.

Home ownership increased even more in the 1980s. Whether it was people's desire to own their homes, or more of a desire to sell off council stock is a long-standing debate and not something we'll get into here. The fact remains that the Right-to-Buy policy was introduced by The Housing Act (1980) which meant that people could now purchase their council homes for a fairly low cost in comparison to the market value. The take-up has been huge. Since the introduction of Right-to-Buy, more than 1.9 million council homes have been sold at a discount, initially of between 33%–50% depending on how long the tenant had been in residence and with guaranteed 100% mortgages from the council. The level of discount offered was reduced in the year 2000 to a maximum of £25,000 due to the slowdown of house building after the recession of the 1990s.

Nevertheless, for the first time in history, property ownership became achievable, not just for the landed gentry, but for the masses too. People began to view their homes as an asset, and a new asset class was born.

In 2012 after another 'recession', the amount of discount on offer was again boosted back up to a maximum discount of £77,900 across England, except in London boroughs where it was £103,900. This increased maximum discount saw numbers of Right-to-Buy purchases by council tenants quadruple from 3,744 sales in 2012–13 to 16,519 sales in 2014–15.

Now, 16,519 houses may seem an insignificant number in the grand scheme of things, but when you consider that the number of new affordable homes delivered in the social rented sector decreased by 61% from 24,550 in 2012–2013 to just 9,590 in 2014–15 *(source: DCLG, Affordable Housing Supply)*, it shows that many people are being encouraged to rent or buy from a new hybrid style landlord/vendor; affordable homes developers instead of waiting for a council house.

The alternative is to stay on the council housing 'waiting' lists, officially known as Choice Based Lettings (or 'No Choice Based Lettings' depending on whether you ask service providers or some service users). The points system for Choice Based Lettings varies by council area, but the fact remains that priority, as it should be, is based on need.

The concept of 'priority need' was established to ensure that pregnant women, homeless families with children and vulnerable adults would be prioritised for assistance. In 2002 the legislation was expanded to include 16 and 17-year-olds, 18 to 20-year-old care leavers and those who are vulnerable due to leaving care; those who have served in the armed forces; those who have spent time in prison; or those fleeing violence or threats of violence.

If you are homeless and don't fall into one of those categories, then it is fair to say that you could be waiting a very long time for social housing through a council or Housing Association. The Private Rental Sector (PRS) is an alternative; so instead of waiting for a council house, people have the option of going to private landlords if they are unable to afford home ownership or simply don't want to own a home. This is where the role of Flippers and property investors is vital, and why you should seriously consider reinvesting some of your flip profits into creating decent Buy-to-Let housing.

The shift away from long-term tenancies in council housing to a more aspirational homeownership structure is a good thing for Flippers. As the supply of council housing is sold off and people on lower wages are encouraged into affordable tenancies/ homeownership, it creates a steady stream of people who, over the decades, are able to move up the housing ladder as the value of their affordable homes rise. In the long term they will be in a position to buy homes at market value from you and us because they have been 'trained' by government to take out a mortgage, which with it comes more perceived responsibility and social mobility than a council or private tenancy.

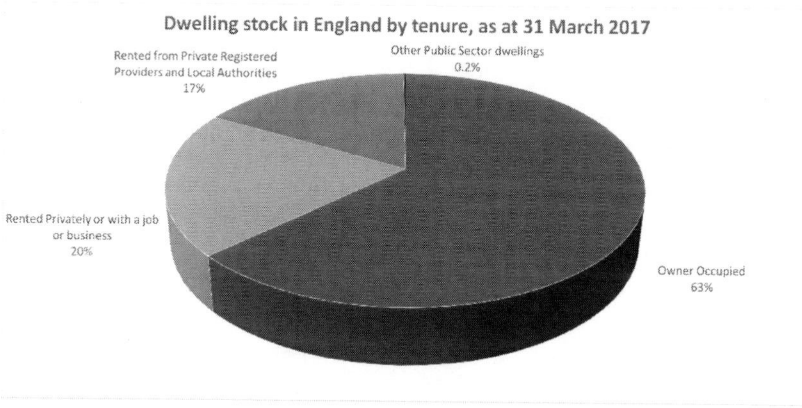

Source: Department for Communities and Local Government. *https://assets.publishing.service.gov.uk/government/uploads/system/uploads/*

attachment_data/file/710382/Dwelling_Stock_Estimates_2017_England.pdf
It is estimated that there are now over 23 million homes in the UK, 63% of which are owner-occupied, so there is definitely a demand for the flips that you will be bringing to market. The number of home owners has risen by more than 1 million between 1997–2016. This shows how people's lifestyles have changed over the years. People in the UK really do like to own their own property if they can.

Despite higher prices, and wages not always keeping pace, people's lifestyles are changing. There is also much more single occupancy nowadays than ever before, which means that more people need somewhere to live and are still buying homes. This is great for you as a Flipper, as you are aiming to create an amazing product (the ideal home) which people want to buy from you. Throughout this book we will teach you where to buy, what to buy, what to do with the property and importantly, how to make a good amount of money along the way. We call it 'chunky money'!

You've probably noticed that Great Britain is surrounded by water. This means that there is a finite resource of space. You might think that this is the reason for there being a housing shortage, but it isn't.

Even though it is the ninth largest island in the world, only 5% of the 60 million acres of land is urbanised, and when you take into account gardens, parks and roads, only 1% of the land mass has houses on it. The rest is countryside, mostly owned by aristocracy, the Church, universities or government.

The reason that there aren't enough properties in the UK, is not only due to the fact that 'we're not building enough', but also because of market forces, population number control and management of our economy.

In 2016–17, 184,000 homes were completed in England. This is more than in recent years, but still below the 2007–2008 pre-recession peak of 200,000.

The UK population is projected to increase by 3.6 million over the next 10 years, from an estimated 65.6 million in mid-2016 to 69.2 million in mid-2026 and is projected to pass 70 million by mid-2029 and be at 72.9 million in mid-2041.

The UK government has relaxed its planning policies recently to stimulate the building of new homes to satisfy demand and close the gap between the quantity of new houses being built and the market demand.

You might wonder why you can't just build more houses. But in reality, it makes sense that there are measures and controls in place, for example, measures that prevent any one person buying a piece of the Forest of Dean, flattening it and turning it into a massive metropolis.

That said, there has been a relaxation in planning laws in recent times in order to encourage smaller scale development. If you can find a flip with a plot, then provided you are in an 'infill village', there are very few restrictions and little reason why planning for up to three houses can be denied if your application is policy compliant.

There is even more potential right now to take advantage of plot space in towns and villages. Anyway, that's going a bit off track, but if you want to know more, then you might want to consider applying to join one of our mastermind groups for more advanced strategies. You can find details of these and other training we offer at *www.tashaandkaren.com*.

It's true that migration into the UK has put additional pressure on the already dwindling housing stock. However, migration has been happening for centuries and will continue for the foreseeable future because our labour market needs it. That doesn't need to be touted as the only reason we have a housing shortage by the newspapers, but it has and will continue to be a headline grabber.

There are a variety of reasons why there is a housing shortage, the result of which means that there will always be demand for the product that you create, provided that you buy it at the right price, spend the right amount on refurbing/renovating it, present the final product to the market and people want to buy it.

Can anyone predict the future?

Flipping property, when done well, creates chunky money. It is a commodity that you can trade and be sure of profit if you do your sums correctly and stay up to date and aware of changes in external factors. By external factors we mean PESTEL changes. A PESTEL (Political, Economic, Social, Technological, Ethical, Legal) analysis is a framework or tool used to analyse and monitor the external marketing environment that have an impact on business. This information is used to identify threats and weaknesses which is then used in a SWOT analysis.

This kind of analysis helps you to determine how these factors will affect the performance of the property market, and how you can take advantage of changes to improve your business in the long-term. As your hobby turns into a business, you will want to understand market trends, review previous years' performances and assess what stage of the property cycle the economy is in.

Here are some things for you to consider:

Political: *"Unless we deal with the housing deficit, we will see house prices keep on rising. Young people will find it even harder to afford* *their own home. The divide between those who inherit wealth and those who don't will become more pronounced."*

Theresa May, Prime Minister (2016)

There will always be political interest in property as housing (shelter) is a basic human need. The tone of information released by government and the opposition parties can influence how your purchasers view the property market. It can also influence their willingness to part with their cash if they feel a downturn is on the horizon. Does this mean that you shouldn't flip in a recession? Definitely not, but you will need to adjust your sails according to the wind.

Economic: The Prime Minister also makes a very interesting comment that could set the scene to better understand the link between housing costs and local economic performance:

"And more and more of the country's money will go into expensive housing instead of more productive investments that generate more economic growth."

Theresa May, Prime Minister (2016)

Social: There is no doubt that society is continuously changing. Taste and fashion are a great example of this change. Your property business will need to take into account changes in tastes and desires in order to stay ahead of the game. A simple example of this are the colours you put in your new property. Whilst pastel colours were popular in the 1950s, there was a colour explosion of orange and yellow flowery wallpapers in the 1960s. Avocado green became popular in the 1980s and then in the 1990s it was white kitchens with ivy wallpaper. Recently we're seeing the uprising of grey and white shades, which is a welcome change from magnolia.

Technological: Imagine being able to put on a Virtual Reality headset in the comfort of your own home and view a house for sale by seemingly walking down the street in real time, through the front door and have the facts and figures about each room scrolling before your very eyes. This time is coming, and it will revolutionise the way we buy and sell houses.

Time is our greatest commodity, and while you may think you have a great flip property, there will need to be a greater emphasis on dressing the property to sell and maximising the information you provide to agents. This will no doubt initially be a paid-for-service and in our opinion, it is less likely that distressed vendors and those with poor flip houses will sign up for the service, so it is vital that you build relationships with those estate agents now to get those properties that don't keep up with the trends. Even with technological advances, there is no substitute for relationship building and face-to-face contact.

Ethical: Since November 2017, HM Land Registry has made available, for free, data on land or property in England and Wales where the registered legal owner is a UK company or corporate body, or an overseas company. The Commercial and Corporate Ownership Data and Overseas Companies Ownership Data contains more than 3 million rows of data and includes the address, company name, price paid and country of incorporation along with other useful information. Visit *https://data.landregistry.gov.uk/* to gain access to the data.

According to an article in the *Evening Standard,* at least £100billion of properties in London alone have been acquired by overseas investors, *"By shadowy corporate structures usually registered in tax havens to hide the buyers' identities... and in some cases has been linked with money laundering and tax evasion".*

Now, this is quite a statement, with a lot of journalistic sensationalism, but underpinning it all is the moral and ethical correctness about the whole situation. In a country with a housing shortage, is it right that properties stand empty or are occupied part of the time by overseas investors and families?

This is not something that has a definitive answer. There are both sides of the argument to consider. If someone can buy something, should they be permitted to? Is it unethical that companies withhold information about their asset ownership, or has the system allowed them to, and therefore their conduct is not considered unethical? Do they have a corporate social responsibility to free up these properties and bring them back to market?

Equally, is it ethical that a London apartment purchased from a council by a British citizen under the Right-to-Buy scheme for £130,000 in 1990, should then be allowed to sell on the open market for £1.2million in 2016, representing an 800% return on the owner's investment? Or is that just the effect of inflation? Whatever your opinion, ethics will always be on people's mind when it comes to property because shelter is a basic human need and it makes for good conversation down the pub or on social media.

Legal: There will always be changes to the legal system in the UK. This is because its foundations were based on an ancient system. When you see a judge or magistrate sitting in court, you are actually looking at the result of 1,000 years of legal evolution.

Today, going on trial in an English and Welsh court is probably not a comfortable experience. But it's far better than trial by ordeal, used until almost the end of the 12th century to determine guilt or innocence in criminal cases.

Under this system, the accused would be forced to pick up a red-hot bar of iron and pluck a stone out of a cauldron of boiling water, or something equally painful and dangerous. If their hand had begun to heal after three days, they were considered to have God on their side, thus proving their innocence. The number of 'not guilty' verdicts recorded by this system is not known.

Hundreds of years of evolution may have resulted in an independent judiciary – but that doesn't mean they were entirely separated from government. Chief Justice Lord Mansfield was in the Cabinet between 1757 and 1765, for example and more recently Lord Cave was Home Secretary for a couple of months at the end of the First World War when he was also a serving Lord of Appeal in Ordinary, or Law Lord.

And until 2006, the Lord Chancellor was part of the executive, the legislature and the judiciary. The Lord Chancellor's role changed drastically on 3rd April 2006 as a result of the Constitutional Reform Act 2005. This latest major change to affect the judiciary has been described as the most significant since Magna Carta. For the first time in its 1,000-year history, the judiciary is officially recognised as a fully independent branch of the government (source: *www.judiciary.gov.uk*).

In recent times we have seen changes of a legal nature in the property industry. Sale and Rent Back (SARB) is a prime example of strategy that has been brought to a halt and there will no doubt be other legal and regulatory changes to the property industry over the course of your Flipping career. They are usually well publicised on forums and by the government as part of their consultation process.

DIYer *vs* Trader – which will you choose?

There are two types of Flippers; the DIYer and the business owner. Plenty of people go from being one to be the other, but through the mentoring we do, we come across people who started out doing the work, then grew a business and rather than getting a project manager in to oversee the refurb and manage the site, they stay in the business and it never really takes off.

You just end up with more people working on site than you need, because you are the one that becomes the surplus, but you're not earning any extra from being there. You just kid yourself that you're needed, and no one can do the bits that you do.

Let us tell you a secret that you already know in your heart of hearts – you're not needed there. You just need to let go of the control and get someone else in to free you up so that you can work on the business rather than in it.

You can't be out looking for the next deals and schmoozing estate agents and joint-venture partners if you are following your builder around with a dustpan and brush or stripping woodchip wallpaper because you think it'll cost too much to get someone else in to do it.

There are plenty of decorators who will quote for this as part of the job and they'll probably sub-contract it to a labourer while they get on with the prep work for the professional finish they're going to give you.

For the first 5 years of our business we were very hands on. In fact, I (Karen) was so hands on I ended up nearly losing a few digits on separate occasions.

If you, like me, sometimes enjoy doing the monotony of repetitive manual jobs then you too probably have a non-dominant hand (the one that you don't write with) that always gets injured. The first time this happened I was clearing ivy off the front of a house with secateurs. I was doing this because I was looking forward to giving the masonry a fresh coat of paint and turning what was a grubby grey ex-local authority house into a white swan.

Unfortunately, in my haste, I misjudged what was ivy and what was glove and snipped through my ring finger; leaving the glove to fill up with bright red blood. Its amazing how your survival instinct kicks in and although I was two storeys up a ladder, I remembered to climb down the ladder rather than jumping backwards off it. Four hours later in A&E, after a tetanus jab and a lot of surgical glue, it was sorted.

That's the benefit of sharp tools – it was a clean cut through the fleshy bit, so no lasting damage done. I did get a lot of grief from friends and family though.

The second time involved an innocent hawthorn bush and a not so blameless set of neighbouring tenants who had let their garden literally become a jungle, which had flowed over the fence into the back garden, taken root in our rental property and invaded pretty much half of it. We only found this out when our tenants had vacated and we went to check the property for the next set. Regardless of the fact that the property should have been fully managed by a national letting agent, the relevant checks weren't done, and the garden was in a state. Our new tenants were due to move in the next day, so I decided to tackle the garden myself. Bad choice.

Hawthorns, as I now know, are notorious for the small backwards barbs on their thorns which, once snapped off, are a pain to get out.

Now imagine a large thorn snapped off in line with the side of the joint of your finger and voilà, you have yourself a foreign body that inflames the joint and prevents your finger from bending.

Six weeks later it still hadn't worked its way out, so I had to be admitted to hospital, go to theatre in a fetching gown, have it surgically removed and have 5 stitches and a big bandage which again made me the butt of jokes with friends and family. The positive from this was that we changed agents and the garden has remained beautiful ever since.

The final hand episode is by far the worst pain I have ever known and on reflection, it was exactly what I needed to make me leverage more.

Later we'll discuss reconfiguring properties to maximise space, and this is exactly what we were doing at one of our properties. We had moved the bathroom from downstairs to upstairs and relocated the kitchen further towards the back of the property. This required the walls to be insulated which we achieved by battening out and then adding insulation, before boarding and skimming the room.

However, in the process of battening out, it was getting late in the day and I was tired. Just one innocuous swing of the hammer resulted in me hitting my finger with the hammer. (The same finger that had recently had its stitches removed from the hawthorn incident.)

Now, a lot of people have hit their finger or thumb with a hammer, used four-letter expletives and got on with it.

However, I managed to smash my hand in such a way that my own finger nail sliced through the thickness of my finger and out the other side. There was claret everywhere and I was in agony.

I remember thinking as I spent 6 hours in A&E waiting for a plastic surgeon to be available to remove the entire nail and stitch the nail bed, that it was time to down tools and find a better way.

If you've ever had stiches in your nail bed, you'll know the absolute agony and inconvenience you go through while it takes 4 months or so for it to grow back. Sometimes we need this pain in order to grow, in more ways than one.

When you're growing a business, you imagine that nobody can do things as well as you. And it's not true. It's just the ego coming through. Everything we do has been learned. Which means that someone else can learn what you do and do it for you.

The good thing about flipping property is that once you've done a couple it becomes almost formulaic. You know what materials to use, where to source them from and who to get to fit them. The only difference if you want to scale and grow the business, is you need more tradespeople involved.

If you are going to trade as a business, and whether you are classed as a trader or not, will very much depend on how your accountant interprets your activity. If you are regularly selling property and using trades – builders, plumbers, electricians, carpenters, tilers, carpet fitters, plasterers etc., then you should be registered with the CIS (Construction Industry Scheme). Your accountant will be able to advise you on this. Visit the CIS website to find out more: *https://www.gov.uk/government/publications/construction-industry-scheme-cis-340*

What is your intention? Are you going to 'tart and turn' a house once a decade to top up your income? If so, your financial advisors *may* say that you could just put it as a capital gain on your tax return. Or are you going to build a sustainable business and flip 10 houses a year? There are economies of scale to be had with buying materials in volume but with it comes responsibility. Trader or DIYer? The choice is yours. And it's great to have that choice.

The key to building a team around you is monetising the time that you would have otherwise spent on site.

If you don't do this, then you might as well be the one stripping the wallpaper or acting as a labourer. (Watching the TV instead of making your time work for you is not the answer.)

Here are some tasks you could be doing instead of being on site:

- Attending auctions
- Attending networking meetings to find JV partners
- Visiting estate agents
- Viewing properties
- Meeting other property Flippers
- Meeting builders on site to look at their other work
- Walking around your local area looking for houses that look empty

- Contacting the council to find out what properties are on their empty homes list and how you can help bring them back into use
- Courting the biggest property landlords in the area and trying to get a JV or temporary job with them to gain experience
- Getting some business cards made
- Building your LinkedIn profile
- List building – collecting business cards, putting them into a spreadsheet and then emailing interesting content to your newly-found contacts (provided they've given you permission and you are GDPR compliant)
- Creating a company website with an email capture section where you give away a report for free in return for contact details (see above regarding GDPR)
- Becoming an ambassador for other companies and getting referral fees or affiliate commission for referring clients. This is more common than you might think.
- Creating a Facebook profile page
- Setting up trade accounts with the builders' yards
- Speaking to friends and family – taking them for dinner/lunch and letting them understand your business better so they can be an ambassador for you
- Attending charity balls

- Attending charity sports days such as golf / rugby / cricket / greyhound racing to sponsor a hole / board / race to use later in your Facebook marketing
- Creating intellectual property – blogging, contributing to Facebook groups, podcasting, positioning yourself as the Expert, or even writing a book!

All of these things will raise your profile and bring you more deals, more knowledge, more contacts and ultimately more cash.

What's your reason 'Why'?

Have a think about what you really want. Most people never do this and it's a real shame. When you start on this journey you may find this part difficult, especially if you haven't thought about it before. This is not a mindset book, you know that already, but it is important to have something to focus on. Don't overthink it, just go with the flow. If you have a day job and love it; that's great. But if you want something different, what is that?

Ask yourself this question:

'If money was no barrier; what would I rather be doing today?'

What is stopping you from doing that right now? Quite often the thing you want to do most you can't do because you need money to pay the bills and to feed the family.

If you do want to leave your job or sack your boss, when are you going to do it? If you don't know the answer to this, then the likelihood is you never will, because you don't have a plan.

If the answer is, *'When I have enough money',* then we are getting somewhere. However, we need to know how much money is enough. Is that £100k, £1m or £100m? A good way to work this out is to know what *net* income you have now on a monthly basis (not what your salary is). What do you actually take home at the end of the month? Take a moment to work this out now.

Let's say that it is £2000 net a month, which is £24k per year. How much do you want to make from your first flip (which will take 6–12 months)? £20k? How about you do two per year; that's £40k. £40k for two flips or a full-time job for £24k?

I know what I would choose.

This may seem like a very simple exercise, but most people don't see that. They just know they need cash next month because the previous month's money has gone and there is more month left than money.

What if you could do two flips alongside your job, put that £40k into the bank and pay yourself £2k a month. That will last you 20 months. You could leave work, continue to flip and still get the same income. Doesn't that make sense?

But why do you want this money? Yes, you might want to leave the pain of a job that you don't like, but what are you going to use the money for? Once you have paid for the essential living costs, what's next? This is one of the most important parts of success because if you don't have a big reason 'why', then why would you put the work in to get there? Think about that for a minute.

It's like going out into the back garden and spending 2 weeks digging a massive hole. What do you have at the end of the process? Well apart from a sore back, you now have a massive hole in your back garden and an equally massive pile of soil.

Why did you do this? If you have no reason why, then there is no point and you probably wouldn't get past the first shovel of dirt.

However, if you wanted to build a swimming pool and that was the most important thing in the world to you, you would go out there every day, dig that hole and at the end of it, create the swimming pool. What you have there is a result, a reason, and your 'Why'.

Write down your reason 'Why'. What would £3k, £5k, £10k, £15k, £20k per month do for you? Write it down now and don't read on until you have done it.

Investing the profits

It is undeniable that Flipping makes big money compared to some other property strategies. By now you've probably noticed that we like to call this '*chunky money*' because the rewards are big enough to give you choice.

You have choice over what to spend it on and whether to spend it all or reinvest it, or just rinse and repeat, ploughing it all straight back into the next deal in order to compound your profits and grow your pot.

Our 'Flip Line', detailed later on, illustrates just what you can do with flipping and how quickly you can grow a portfolio or whatever is your preferred strategy.

Money for deposits

You may like to do a mixture of investment and reward spending. But whether you're into Single Lets, HMOs, Serviced Accommodation, Lease Options, Rent-to-Rent, Commercial Property or other strategy, the profits from flipping can be used to fund your purchases in full, or give you deposit money in order to secure a mortgage or bank finance on the rest of the purchase.

Flipping properties will also make you more visible to estate agents and more likely to bring deals to you first because they like repeat business.

Other property strategies are geared up for investment and long-term returns rather than significant short-term gains. If you buy single lets, then your intention upon purchase is to make a rental surplus. You should aim for £200 profit a month as a minimum, taking into account the cost of maintenance, mortgage, management and voids (plus service charges and ground rent if the property is leasehold). Buy-to-Let investors making £200 profit a month will earn around £2400 a year from a single let, if nothing goes wrong, and they will also hope to gain asset value over time but shouldn't rely on it.

Traders on the other hand however will forgo the long-term income in favour of short-term chunky money upon the sale of the property.

This is how many investors have started out. They buy and sell a property and then invest the profits into a rental portfolio.

If building an asset base is important to you, then the next section details the investment strategies to consider.

The following property investment strategies are used for cashflow and capital appreciation with the exception of Rent-to-Rent, which is purely a cashflow strategy unless you can secure the property on an Option agreement.

Single buy-to-let property: These can be any type of residential properties which are typically rented out on a 6-month assured shorthold tenancy (AST) to one person or family unit. There is currently consultation underway to extend the minimum length of tenancies, but at present most new tenants are offered an initial fixed period of 6 or 12 months. These properties can be self-managed or let out through a letting agency. A good cash flowing single let should pay you between £200–£300 per calendar month as a minimum. The tenant will pay the landlord monthly rent and will also be responsible for all of the monthly bills. The landlord will need to pay any mortgage or loan on the property and make sure that it is properly insured.

The cash you need for this strategy is for the mortgage deposit (around 25% of the purchase price, depending on your circumstances), money for stamp duty and refurbishment if required and some cash for application fees, legal fees and insurance. You can get a standard buy-to-let mortgage to finance your purchase.

Multi-let property (house in multiple occupancy or HMO): These are usually larger properties which are let out by the room, with multiple tenancy agreements or license agreements. For example, if the property has 6 bedrooms, each bedroom will have a lock on the door and might contain an ensuite bathroom. If there is no ensuite, then shared bathrooms are provided. There is also a shared kitchen / dining space and sometimes a separate shared lounge too. Each tenant will pay one rental payment per month, often but not always, inclusive of the monthly bills. Utilities are the responsibility of the landlord/owner of the property. The landlord pays any loan/mortgage on the property plus all of the bills, including gas, electric, water, council tax, and insurance.

High-end versions of these properties often come with a weekly cleaner and gardener which again is paid for by the landlord. Cashflow for HMO will vary dramatically as you can have any size from a 2 bed 'Mini-Mo', and up to as many occupants as you like as long as you are within the rules and regulations of the area you invest in. Typically, a 6-bed HMO should give you £800–£1500 per calendar month net profit.

The cash you need for this strategy is for the mortgage deposit (approximately 30% of the purchase price, again depending on your circumstances), stamp duty, plus money for refurbishment if it's already a HMO, or the full conversion money if you are turning a family home into a HMO. The cost of conversion can vary depending on the works required, but we regularly spend £50k–60k on converting houses into HMOs. As with a single let, you'll need cash for application fees, legal fees and insurance. You'll also need cash to fund the purchase of the furniture as HMOs are usually fully furnished by the landlord. You'll need a specialist HMO mortgage product to run larger HMOs and should use a specialist broker to get the best deal in terms of interest rate, fixed term of the loan, permission for intended works and length of the borrowing.

Commercial units: Buying commercial units to let out to businesses can be a good long-term investment as you can agree long leases, and that the lease holder takes care of all maintenance of the property on a Full-Repairing-and-Insuring (FRI) lease. Commercial units are often a case of 'let it and forget it', provided that you secure a decent tenant and remember to negotiate a good lease with break clauses and periodic rent increases included as standard.

For this strategy, you'll need cash for either the full purchase price, or just a deposit if you're getting bank lending. The amount of deposit will vary depending on the type of commercial unit you purchase, and the usual application and legal fees will apply.

Serviced Accommodation: The meteoric rise of Airbnb and Booking.com has given holiday makers and travellers more choice over where to stay. Traditionally, people looking for overnight accommodation would be restricted to staying at hotels or guesthouses. The rise of Serviced Accommodation has turned this on its head and people are now able to book a room for the night, or even a whole property.

It often pays to have a two-night minimum stay to bring down the cost of cleaning and bedding etc. This strategy is great for cashflow if you can get the systems in place and have a great location and quality rooms/properties to let out. You need to make sure that all of the cleaning, bed changing, key collection and drop off is organized very well, and that the booking system and channel manager is in place.

For this strategy, you will need money for the purchase price or deposit, plus lending and refurbishment costs which can be similar to a HMO once you've taken account of fully renovating and furnishing the property to achieve the standard required for a nightly let room or whole property.

Rent-to-Rent: Rent-to-Rent or Corporate Letting is where you rent a property from another landlord and sub-let it, with their permission. It is normal to pay the owner a guaranteed rent for a number of months or years and then rent out the rooms individually in the style of a HMO or turn it into Serviced Accommodation. As with a standard HMO or SA unit you will be responsible for the bills (unless agreed otherwise with the owner). You will also need to make agreements with the owner about who will manage maintenance issues.

Cashflow with this strategy can be similar to a standard HMO or SA unit. The difference is you aren't actually buying the property, and therefore don't have the upfront purchasing costs. You also never own it or benefit from the capital appreciation unless you secure it on an Option Agreement.

This strategy is popular with people who either don't want, or haven't got the cash required, to own properties. The conversion costs to make it a multi-let will sometimes be paid by the landlord, as you don't own the property and don't want to spend too much on someone else's asset.

You should ask the owner to help out with funding any improvements, either up front or by reducing the rent accordingly if you pay for them. A good selling/negotiating point is that the improvements to the property actually helps to increase the value.

Evergreen strategy

Flipping works in every stage of the property market cycle, you just need to adjust accordingly to the market conditions. We have been involved in property since 2006. During this time, we have seen the market at its peak, its lows and everything in between.

If you understand the market cycle and respect that things will change, opinions will vary and buyers will be more plentiful sometimes and less so at others, then you are well on your way to becoming a successful Flipper. If you know what to buy, where to buy and what to do for maximum returns, then you will get a result every time.

An 'in and out' strategy

Flipping is short term. What we mean by this is that you only own the property for a short amount of time. While interest rates might be going up and down and affecting the Buy-to-Let market and people with residential mortgages, the short-term nature of any borrowing you have on a flip gives you more confidence that the repayments won't vary.

When investors buy a Buy-to-Let property, the term of the loan is usually 25 years. Over the 25 years, interest rates will almost certainly change, sometimes in the borrower's favour and sometimes working against them. This uncertainty can be quite daunting for new investors and may put some people off altogether.

This needn't be the case because when interest rates increase, so can rents.

When interest rates drop, there are higher profit margins and the opportunity to pay down loans with the surplus or put it away for a rainy day. You can also fix the interest rate for a certain amount of time too.

With flipping, you will buy, renovate and sell the property within a year and any bank lending will usually be on a fixed rate because neither you nor they want the loan to drag on. The fixed interest rates are normally higher than that of a Buy-to-Let, which is ok, provided that you've done your numbers correctly and factored this in from the start.

No tenants

Tenants are a necessary part of owning Buy-to-Lets and HMOs. You will need tenants, and we do love (most of) our tenants, but with tenants comes extra challenges. We have many tenants across our portfolio and while 95% of the time they are considerate people, you always get the odd one who doesn't pay the rent or accidentally drives their car into the front of the house. Yes, seriously, that has happened.

When flipping property there are NO tenants. The last thing you want is to do a full refurb and then put tenants in while it is on the market.

The first reason is that you will need to offer them, at a minimum, a 6-month tenancy.

Secondly, if a potential tenant knows that you actually want to sell the property then they are less likely to sign up for a 6-month tenancy and then have to move again in a short space of time.

But the main reason is that once you move tenants in, the property loses its brand-new feel and appeal. The carpets get dirty, the kitchen gets a bit greasy and the tile grout in the shower never looks pure white again.

Even the most considerate of tenants who instructs a professional cleaning company to clean the property at the end of the tenancy will never get it immaculately clean, and that's what buyers want. They want to move into a freshly decorated house with a new kitchen and bathroom. This is what gets you a premium price, so don't be tempted by tenants for the couple of months between completing the works and meeting the 6-month rule (this is the duration of ownership required by some banks before lending to your potential purchasers).

Easy to understand exit strategy

There is literally nothing simpler to understand or explain to a Joint Venture partner than the Buy-to-Sell model. You buy a property, renovate it and sell it. Once the property is sold, the profits are shared out in accordance with any loan agreements you have put in place and everyone is free to move on or go again. It's such an easy strategy to understand and explain that it surprises me that more people aren't doing it. Thanks to the simplicity of it, you will attract more JV partners. JV partners love flips. Fact.

Most people live in or have lived in a house, so they understand the principle of refurbishing and making it nicer. Even if they've only lived there as a tenant.

Of those people who live in a house, a percentage have purchased one. It's easy for them to understand what you are doing in the JV and then appreciate the certainty of the exit route i.e. the sale.

Job replacing profits

Chunky money from flips can replace or supplement your income; it's just about taking action and making the decision to do something.

What people sometimes forget is while the average UK salary in 2017 was approximately £28k (source: ONS.gov.uk), take home pay from that after deductions for National Insurance and Income Tax puts the take home figure nearer to £22k.

This, as a minimum 'Return On Time Invested', is entirely achievable through flipping if you have a systemised, structured flipping business.

Time, choice, freedom and fun

Aside from the tangible benefits of flipping property, it can actually be a fun and rewarding activity to do.

We've made great relationships with our tradespeople and it's great to be on site with them because they all take pride in their work and are a joy to be around. If you've ever been in a manual job, you'll appreciate the banter and goodwill that people have with each other if the right environment is created.

We like to think that we attract the right kind of people by having a can-do attitude and cutting people a bit of slack when they need it. Everyone is doing the best they can at any given time. Your best will vary from day to day, as will that of the people who you choose to work with.

With flipping, projects take a little longer than your standard Buy-to-Let refurb and you'll soon get to know who you want on your sites and who doesn't quite fit.

It's nice to have that choice and freedom to have the right people there at the right time, rather than sitting in an office dreaming of the world that's outside.

Flipping gives you the variety and challenges that every human needs, so it makes complete sense to have it in your life.

Your level of involvement is entirely up to you. If being creative and designing floorplans is your thing, then focus on that. If you love manual tasks, there are lots of them to get stuck in with. If finding the deals is more for you, then great, negotiation is key to getting properties at a good price. If you like keeping a tight grip on spreadsheets and the purse strings, then do that.

There is such a variety of roles with a flip that one or more of them is likely to float your boat. Then it's about getting the right team around you to do the rest.

What could you spend the money on?

Because flips give you chunky money, you have the choice to invest into more flips, buy assets which will continue to pay you and increase in value forever, or a mix of the two.

Let us show you how you could use flips to build a portfolio:

Peter has £100,000 in cash and is receiving 2% interest per year from the bank. At the end of the year Peter has earned £2,000 interest, minus bank fees and any taxes due.

You meet Peter through a family friend and he asks what you do.

Subject to you and/or your company being PS13/3 compliant (you can find more details about how this may affect you here: www.fca.org.uk/publication/policy/ps13-03.pdf), you tell him about the joint ventures that you do with other investors and your flip strategy.

It goes something like this:

"It's very straightforward. I will purchase a property with your cash, renovate the property and put it back on the market for sale. I will pay you an interest rate of 5%. At the end of the process you will get your £100,000 plus £5,000 interest with no fees or deductions other than any taxes you would normally pay. How does that sound?"

Peter is excited by this and agrees.

You buy a property for £74,000 purchase price and with stamp duty, legal fees, future taxes and refurb costs, it's all in for about £100,000. 6 months later, the property sells for £125,000. You return Peter's £100,000 plus £5,000 interest and have about £20,000 left for yourself.

You decide to purchase a single Buy-to-Let property using some or all of the £20,000 for the deposit, stamp duty, fees and a light refurb. If it's a more expensive property, then you top up the pot with some of your own cash from another flip or savings.

Peter has his money back but is still only getting 2% at the bank so says to you, "*Do you have any more deals like that last one?*"

You do, and so you repeat the process and end up buying another single Buy-to-Let with the profits. This is repeated a third time, however this third time you are getting much better at this and you buy in a better area for a better price. Your refurb is cheaper and you keep the costs lower by being more experienced. This time you make £30,000 profit which allows you to purchase a small HMO as an asset, while Peter gets his money and interest back.

Over the space of three deals you have made a friend in Peter because instead of making £6,000 in the bank (minus fees) he has made £15,000 by investing with you.

You may have started with no money but had the knowledge, motivation and enthusiasm and as a result you now have three assets in your portfolio. Your two single-lets bring in £4,800 per year (£200 per calendar month each) and your HMO brings in £7,200 per year (£600pcm), which in total gives you £12,000 per year.

Your portfolio still has the £70,000 deposit money stored as equity and has increased in value because you undertook a light refurb after buying the rental properties. You also purchased them at less than market value because you knew what to buy and where to buy, which gives you an additional equity of £60,000.

So you see, you can generate £142,000 in a relatively short space of time by borrowing other people's money, making more money for them than they would have received in the bank and by investing the profits into building your own portfolio.

See the next diagram for a more visual display of how this works.

THE FLIP LINE

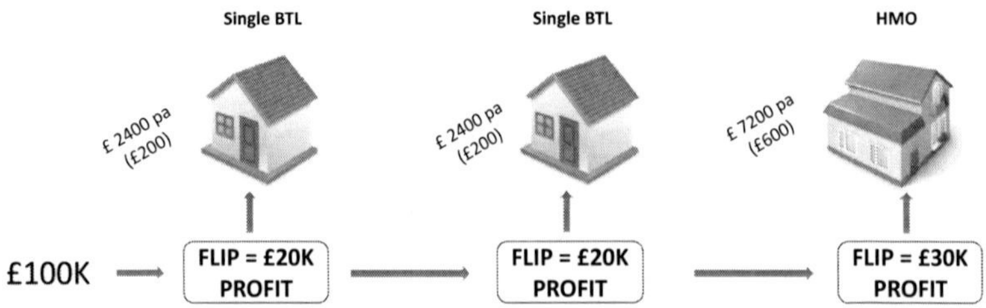

- ❑ £70K profit – now invested in assets
- ❑ 3 additional assets – equity additional £60K
- ❑ Cashflow from 3 properties – **£12,000 pa**
- ❑ TOTAL **£142K**

It's not rocket science, it's just not something they taught us and perhaps you in school.

"Formal education will make you a living;

self-education will make you a fortune" (Jim Rohn)

Trading is a process that anyone can learn and implement, but most people will never seek out this information.

The same principle applies to trading shares, stock, watches, wine and classic cars. You just need to invest the profits into something that gives you recurring income and you will be on the road to sustainable wealth.

Section 3: The fundamentals of sourcing and assessing a property's potential

Section 3: The fundamentals of sourcing and assessing potential.

Keeping it local

Where should you flip property? Well, we think the short answer if you are in the UK… is in the UK. We don't advocate buying and selling property abroad unless you have experience in those property markets and even if you do, it is definitely a case of 'Buyer Beware'.

Make sure to have a valid Last Will & Testament in every country where you own property if you do have them overseas. The legal systems abroad vary massively from the UK and unless you have a base there or detailed knowledge of a country, we would stay well clear.

It's often tempting when you go abroad to imagine yourself owning a property there, but the reality is that it's an emotional decision you're making whilst relaxing with friends or family.

Just because something is cheap in comparison to home, it doesn't make it a sound investment. Imagine seeing a property advertised at the side of the highway in Florida for $50,000. You do some quick sums and work out that's just £30,000. That's cheap!

Imagine all of the holiday makers you could rent it out to – after all, you looked for ages to find a villa for your trip.

Wrong! $50,000 is cheap. It's too cheap, which means it'll be well away from the parks, transport links and will be more of a shack than the air-conditioned 3 bed condo with a swimming pool that you and the rest of the holidaymakers searched for and could get within budget.

By the time you've paid for cleaning, launderers, maintenance, pool cleaners and management and found that it was too good to be true and no one wants to stay in your shack, it's too late and you will regret ever purchasing the damn place.

And then you'll advertise it on the side of the highway in the hope of snaring another emotional holidaymaker with a bit of spare cash because you can't afford to use a realtor to sell it for you. And the cycle goes on.

The golden rule of flipping is sticking to an area you know or picking a new area and sticking to that area and getting to know it well. There are some people who advocate flipping remotely and sourcing properties anywhere in the country to flip, but again, buyer beware.

We flip properties that are within 30 minutes of our home. Or we'll invest with another experienced Flipper and simply fund a flip in their area where they are the local expert and have the systems and teams set up to get on with the job.

By focussing on one area, you build specific relationships with specific agents and tradespeople. Spreading yourself across too wide a geographical area will lead to a scatter gun approach. Pick one area and go deep rather than wide. It'll focus your mind and improve your margins.

So will flipping work in your area? The answer is always YES. There are properties on your doorstep right now which are ready for you to make chunky money from.

However, you need to know exactly what you are looking for to make that profit. Cheap properties are not always the answer. It may look like an amazing deal, but do your due diligence and make a rational decision rather than an emotional one.

Conservation Areas & Article 4 Directives: When you think about doing a flip property, you want the easiest route possible, and some of the fundamental research that can be done, even before you offer on a property is around Article 4 areas. Some people think this is just to do with HMOs, but it's not.

An Article 4 directive can be introduced on any property, but it is most commonly found on domestic dwellings located within conservation areas. When implemented, they can withdraw certain permitted development rights. You can go onto your local council website, depending on the area you will be flipping in, and they should have a list of all of the properties that have Article 4 directives.

This is a key piece of research, because if you are thinking about choosing one property over another when you are assessing deals, one of them might require you to have like-for-like windows made out of timber for example, which could add significant costs to the project.

That is not to say that you would not choose a property based in an Article 4 area, you just need to be aware before you start the project that there will be certain hoops to jump through in order to please the council.

You should definitely not undertake works on a property that has Article 4 directives without letting the council know first, as this will cause problems for you when you come to sell the property down the line.

If a house has an Article 4 directive, this means you can make certain alterations to the property, but you might require full planning permission in order to do so.

The information that you receive from the council will give different classes that apply to the Article 4 directive. An example may be that you find that you are not allowed to paint or alter the exterior of a building if it can be viewed directly from the street without full planning permission.

If that is the case, and it is going to add at least 8 weeks to your project, this can have real implications on your budget. You can also get information from your council, or local council website about the conservation areas that are around. Conservation areas tend to be the base for nicer houses, so they have extra perceived value when you come to sell the property, but you will need to download the maps from your council website so that you are well informed as to where these areas are, and this is a really simple thing to do that some people will overlook.

What do you think is the most important part to flipping? Well, it's making sure you can sell the property in the end. It really is that simple. You need to create a product that people want. And then you need to present it to them in the best condition you can in order to leave them with no doubts or concerns about the property after the very first viewing.

How to create an abundance of opportunities

If you're just starting out in property, you may *feel* that all the good deals have gone.

We often hear things like, "*There are loads of other people wanting the same deals*", "I *can't get the relationship with the agents*" and "*It's too late for me*". But when is the best time to start investing in property? The answer is always NOW.

Yes, it would be great to go back to 1984 when the average price was around £30k but unfortunately, we don't have a time machine or a magic wand. All we have and always will have is NOW, not yesterday, not tomorrow. NOW is the time, so what are you waiting for? Do it NOW!

From the start of your investment journey, whether that's now or in the past, you must create a pipeline system from Day 1.

So what is a pipeline system? Well let's say you start to view possible flip properties now.

You may be viewing 10, 20, 30+ properties per month. Can you remember them all?

Can you even remember what price you offered? It's highly unlikely.

In the same way that you'll need to keep a record of the property viewings you do, and complete a Viewing Checklist (which we cover in detail later on), you also need another spreadsheet to record just the top line details of each property you view, with a column for the next action needed.

Some of the best deals you will ever get are the ones which are in your pipeline.

This can be from a property you viewed 4, 6, 8, or 12+ months ago. The deal may have fallen through four times since you viewed it and the estate agent is desperate to shift this property. Your name is on their list as a previous viewer and you probably even offered at the time.

You should record which properties you viewed, when you viewed them, and what you offered, as it can be very embarrassing to get a call from the agent to discuss a property you viewed and you don't remember the details.

When you are viewing lots of properties, it's impossible to remember them all and remember what you offered. By having this information on file, you can confidently say what you offered and when, and that you are still interested.

With the pain of the time lapse since your offer, you may even get a better deal.

Also, within your pipeline, (in the action section) you can schedule follow-up phone calls and follow-up drive-bys. If you offered on a property and you believe it was sold, make a note to check sold house prices after 6 months on Mouseprice.com, Rightmove.co.uk, Nethouseprices.com or your preferred house price data website.

If it shows a recent sold price then you can cross that property off of your list and if not; it may well be worth a call to the agent to see what's happening.

All of these tasks are also easy to leverage out to other people, freeing you up for more important tasks.

Points to include in your data capture:

- Date –> the date you found the property
- Description / location
- Type –> TERR / MIDTERR / DET / BUNG /FLAT
- Price –> asking price
- Postcode –> the property postcode
- Status –> available or SOLD STC
- Agent –> name and phone number of selling agent
- Date(s) viewed -> record first viewing / second viewing etc
- URL –> copy of the online URL (full website address)
- ACTION –> online research / phone agent / drive-by / leaflet / offer (and what is was)

- OUTCOME –>
- NEXT ACTION –>
- NEXT OUTCOME –>

Continue this until the last OUTCOME = SOLD!

Inside the mind of a trader

When we started out on our property journey it was as simple as a conversation over dinner one night.

We were both working long hours – Tasha as an IT consultant, travelling all over the UK and Karen as a Project Manager.

We just decided to buy a property to give us something to do. We didn't know at that time whether we were going to rent it out or sell it.

We searched on the internet for something that we could 'do up' in our spare time, bought our first terrace house and set about bringing it into the 21st century.

We purchased it from a guy who was getting on in life and wanted to move into a retirement property so that he could be less isolated and better equipped for being supported as he got older.

You might be able to imagine the condition of the property, but let me describe it so that you can get a feel for the excitement you too can feel about your first property purchase.

Imagine a row of terrace houses. You walk down the road and as you look to your left you see a house that looks a bit different to the others. It's not falling down, it's not in a bad state, but it looks a bit tired and grey.

You walk down the path and as you look around the small front garden you see a well-kept slabbed area, a little window box and some specimen roses planted in the borders.

You look up at the windows and see net curtains with a simple ornament centred behind each one. You walk up to the door and see a white ceramic house number plate with dark blue trim and blue painted numbers.

You reach forward to press the doorbell and as you do, you hear not a bell, but a little tune. I'm sure you can already picture the kind of person who lives here.

The door opens, and you see a smiley lady who welcomes you in. It's not the home owner, it's the estate agent, but you're already betting that the owner is there too. And sure enough he is.

As you walk through the front door, you see the stairs dead ahead of you and the living room to the right. You walk into the living room and he's there, sat in his favourite arm chair and as you go in he gets up to greet you. It takes a few seconds as he is getting on in his years and you feel that he is doing the right thing, moving into accommodation that can meet his needs and give him more company as he gets older.

He says, "*I've lived here for 56 years Love. If there's anything you'd like to know, just ask*". And there it is. Confirmation that the rest of the house will probably be as well maintained as the lounge is and in a certain style.

You suspect that you're setting out on a journey back in history through the different decades of décor. You can already imagine what the rest of the house is like. Net curtains at every window, swirly carpets for as far as the eye can see and glossed surfaces. But not white gloss, coloured gloss, on the door frames, on the skirting boards and on the bannister. It can only be described as a sort of beige or taupe, but it's everywhere.

You walk through from the living room into the dining room and there on the right is an oval shaped teak table with four chairs. On the table is a lace doily big enough to wrap a small child in and in the middle of the table is a simple pot plant.

You carry on through to the kitchen and look around. Its simple and you can tell that the owner has lived on his own for some time.

You walk through the kitchen and see that the cabinets haven't been replaced since the seventies. The cooker is a white enamel one, the type that you might see in a rental property with an oven with hob on top with black rings and then a grill over the top of it, with a pull-out grill tray which has tin foil on it. The stainless-steel sink opposite is immaculately clean, but when the light catches it you see the many tiny scratches from years of being cleaned with a Brillo pad. He is a house-proud man.

There are flying ducks on the wall and the kitchen floor has carpet tiles with slightly more colour around the edges than on the main thoroughfare.

You continue your journey through the kitchen to the last room which is the bathroom. It is separated into two rooms. As you look ahead at both rooms you see a toilet and basin on the left and a bath in the room on the right. Next to the bath is a small chair with a straw hat on it. You smile and wonder briefly if it gets sunny in that room and there's a chance of sun burning your ears whilst taking a bath.

This is good because when you turn around to proceed through the house, you see that the owner has come to see if you have any questions and ask if he can show you the garden.

Because you are smiling about the hat, he smiles, and you make a connection. You predict that the fact that he is offering to show you the garden means that it's not a jungle. And you're right.

You go outside from the door in the kitchen, down the little path that goes past the kitchen and bathroom and stand both admiring the long garden.

The owner tells you about the plants in the borders and how to take the bins out past the neighbour's house and who has right of way across the path.

You are particularly pleased because you notice at the end of the garden there is plenty of room to develop off-road parking which can be accessed from the road behind for a couple of vehicles without compromising what will be a straight forward garden to maintain.

You go back inside the house and proceed back through the dining room, through the lounge and up the stairs. As you go up the stairs, past the painted china plates with little scenes of country villages on the wall, you notice the woodchip wallpaper which is a sign of things to come. You hope that it's not everywhere, but inevitably, it is. It's been painted in a variety of colours.

One bedroom is peach while the other is lime green. The master bedroom however has green and white stripy wallpaper with a small gold stripe in it. The carpet in this room is green and fluffy. As you look around you count up the number of sockets and check out the light switches. You're pleased to see that they've been attended to recently.

You walk back from the master bedroom into the back bedroom and open the window. You take a quick look up and down the street to check out the neighbours' properties and notice that they're all the same. Everyone is taking care of the of gardens. You also see that no one has any extensions or conservatories.

You wander back down the stairs making a mental note of everything you pass and quickly think of some questions to ask the agent. “When was the boiler last serviced?” “Are the neighbours nice?” “What are the local shops like?” The agent answers your questions and you thank the owner for showing you around his home.

As you leave the property the neighbours are out in their front garden, so you smile and say “Hello”, before walking down the path, around the corner and back to your car.

As you get in the car you get that nervous feeling in your stomach, that feeling that something good is about to happen. And your brain says, ‘*let’s buy it!*’

And there are thousands of properties like this in the UK. It’s an unfortunate fact of life that everyone gets older, and as they do, their tastes in décor and furniture will remain as a nod to the past.

You see, people only do the things to their homes that they need. They don’t reconfigure to get the best out of the space, and they don’t keep up with the trends in interior design.

They are functional homes that enable them to bring up their families and enjoy the space. At some point their needs will change and they will move on. They are no longer the custodian of that property, but you could be for a short time whilst bringing it up to the modern-day desires and making a profit from the process.

This book has been designed to inspire you to see the possibility. You'll find stories galore and hint and tips to make your journey into flipping a fun one. You don't have to be hands on either, but you do need to be passionate about property.

So where to begin? Well, you'll need to master some fundamentals in order to be a successful Flipper:

1. Where to look
2. What to buy
3. Who to sell it to
4. What to do to it

There are some fundamental things to consider when establishing whether a property is 'a deal' or not. Some people get overly enthusiastic about having 'a deal' when in fact all they've done is found a property which may or may not be a deal once they've done their due diligence. These are some of the things that your purchaser might be looking for nearby, and looking to avoid when buying a renovated property from you:

Amenities that people want:

- Shops (but not directly next door)
- Bus stop
- Train station
- Major road links
- Cycle paths
- Playground
- Park
- Swimming pool
- Leisure facilities – gym, bars, cinema, bowling
- Good schools– which is the best?
- Clubs for older people
- Neighbourhood watch
- Located in a designated public place (no alcohol in street)
- Dog walking route nearby
- Major employers
- Sports clubs – football pitches
- Golf course (preferably not crazy!)
- Landmarks and places of interest

What people do not want:

- Landfill sites

- High crime areas
- High ratio of social housing
- Industrial areas
- Busy dual carriageway
- Neighbours from hell
- Litter
- Anti-social behaviour
- Student areas
- Takeaways next door
- Double yellow lines everywhere
- Pub/nightclub next door
- Dog poo
- Lack of parking

Location, location, location, location

Once you have decided to take on flipping as your strategy, you then need to research the area to find out where the best places are to flip.

If you grew up in the area or have lived there for a long time, then you are already half way there as you already have good knowledge of your area. Wherever you grew up, you will remember people saying things like, "*That street is a bit dodgy*" … "*I wouldn't walk in that area at night*" …. "*The people down there are strange.*"

It's all just local gossip, however reputations stick for quite a long time and if an area is known for being a bit dodgy, then it is NOT a flip area. It may be an amazing deal and a property may cost just £25,000, however if you can't sell it because of its location, then you may as well throw away the £25,000 and save yourself lots of time and energy.

Areas do change. Places benefit from regeneration over time and you need to be aware of what is happening and when. That way you can stay ahead of the game and get an early mover advantage in areas that other people aren't looking at or don't yet see the potential in.

When deciding which area to buy in, a fundamental consideration is the person who is going to purchase it from you. If you visit an area and are worried that the wheels might not be on your car when you get back to it, don't buy it.

If you drive down a street during the day and half of the residents are sitting out in their front gardens in white string vests, drinking cider from 2 litre blue plastic bottles and yelling at each other; don't buy it to flip.

That said, there aren't many of these streets in the UK and even if you do end up finding a deal in one of these locations, it doesn't mean that you can't do something with a house there. It will just take longer to sell it or realise the true bricks and mortar valuation because of the level of poverty or deprivation, so it might be ideal instead as a rental property if your preferred tenant type is people on Local Housing Allowance or Universal Credit.

Get a map of your flip area (order one now!) and start to highlight 'nice' places with a highlighter pen. Circle the places and neighbourhoods where people really aspire to live. A good place to start are places where you would like to live.

Get to know these areas by driving, walking or cycling around them. This may be difficult but one of the things we do a lot is to visit the local restaurants and pubs in the area.

Pubs, wine bars and cafés at the heart of the community are places where people go to meet up and relax. If you're nervous at the start of your property journey, just take a newspaper with you and order a drink while you sit there and absorb the hustle and bustle of the area.

Then you can start to have conversations with local people who may have lived there for many years. These people will be more than happy to tell you the best places, the not so nice places, who used to live where and why. They may even know of a property that looks tired, one that's been sitting empty for years or someone who needs to move fast.

Off market deals are amazing and even in this day and age of people communicating through their phones, apps or games, there is still and always will be a proportion of people who communicate with each other in the traditional way – face to face. Be one of those people.

Start to think about what's important to people who are looking for a house to buy and settle down into for at least a few years. Do they want to live by the side of a motorway? Do you think that may put people off buying your property? Yes, of course it will. However, we have seen amateurs buying these properties and doing great refurbs, only to limit their purchaser market because only a very small amount of people would like to live by a motorway.

People need to be able to get to places easily, but the '*want'* emotion will always override the '*need*' emotion if there is a compromise to be had and they will want to live in a nice location.

Think about transport links including main roads, train stations, tube stations, bus stops and even airports. Schools are another big pull for people looking to move. When people have children, they quite often need a bigger house as that bachelor / bachelorette city flat just isn't practical anymore. They want their children to go to a great school and they will often do whatever it takes to get them into a particular school. They want to do the best for them.

We recently learned that the parents of one of the students at Karen's school had pretended that they were getting divorced and that the Dad had moved into a rented property opposite the school they wanted their children to go to in order to get a guaranteed place. They weren't separating at all, they just felt that taking out a six-month tenancy in order to get their children into that secondary school for the next 7 years was worth paying the rent and utilities for 6 months. It worked, the school fell for it and their application was approved. The whole family lived about 7 miles away in a different town and they probably still do to this day.

A simple Google search of schools in the area will quickly show you where people want to place their children, and it will also show you the catchment area for that school. Rightmove also gives you this data. You should add this layer of information to your map as potentially a great flipzone area.

Understanding your potential purchasers

So now you know what kind of area to look in, let's look at how to find the right property. A nice shiny renovated house that someone can move into, maybe add a coat of paint to, isn't a flip. You need to find something that needs modernisation or that you can add value to.

When looking at properties, you firstly need to think about location as we've just covered. Next, who is going to buy this property, and what do they want?

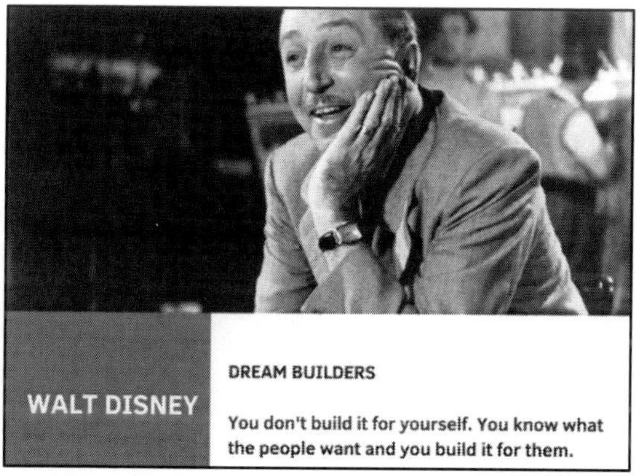

If you buy a bungalow, carry out a loft conversion and garage conversion turning it into a games room, then you realise the target purchasers are mostly likely going to be an elderly couple who don't want stairs and want to put their car in the garage, then you have a problem.

You may have created a great property, but in the wrong location which will limit the number of people who will want to buy it.

You must research and be confident that you know who your target purchasers are and what they want from a property in that location.

The following table is not an exhaustive list and there is certainly cross-over of pros and cons between the different property types, so we have avoided duplication and given you some things to consider when evaluating which property types you will focus on.

Property types

Type	**Pros**	Cons
Flat/ Maisonette	• Smaller, cheaper refurb • City centre locations, so good demand • Proximity to amenities – selling point • Leasehold – fewer structural costs unless asked to contribute • Potential for resolving freeholder issues • Potential for extending lease and adding value • Allocated parking	• Access for refurb – stairs/communal • Noise – close to neighbours • Leasehold – length left • Management/ service charges • Absentee freeholders • Might need permission for works • Existing tenant/owner stereotypes

		• Parking issues if city centre
Bungalow	• Commands higher price per sqm • No stairs for refurb • High demand • Potential for loft conversions • Cash purchasers from downsizing	• Higher purchase price outlay • More competition when buying • Fixed ceiling price • Non-standard construction in some areas
Terraced	• Easy to get price comparables • Plot potential if end terrace • Warmer property if mid-terrace • Fewer windows to replace! • Repeatable cookie cutter strategy	• Competition from buy-to-let investors and first-time buyers • Is there enough on street parking? • Boundaries/rights of access may have changed over time • Ceiling price
Semi detached	• Often a larger garden than terraced house • More space for layout changes • Only one set of neighbours to deal with • Potential for off-road parking	• Neighbours may be opposed to major works and disruption • Exterior finish may be an issue if it is too different from the neighbour's side
Detached	• More space for layout changes • Greater potential for extensions – 8m under permitted development • Plot potential	• Generally more purchase money/SDLT required • Cost of refurb can be higher

Town House	• Proximity to amenities – selling point • Newer properties – fewer refurb issues to resolve especially if it's a repossession	• Multiple floors • Tends to be newer so less potential to add value • Parking issues • PD restrictions

We have built our business by focussing on properties that mainly meet the following criteria:

- Worst house in the best street
- Two/Three-bed properties
- Terraced/Semi/Detached/Bungalow (not usually flats)
- Older style houses – ideally pre-1960's but definitely no new builds under 10 years old.
- Garden and potential for off-road parking
- Under £300k to purchase.

We often hear people say that there aren't any houses in their area for this price bracket, but it simply isn't true.

You can find out the affordability of houses per region by using the BBC Affordability Calculator at: *http://www.bbc.co.uk/news/business-23234033*.

There are houses like this everywhere and when you truly believe this and focus on making it your mission to find them, you will get deals.

We focus on these types of property because they are the ones that have most potential for the smallest amount of time-consuming work.

That's not to say you can't add massive value by adding an extension/loft conversion/basement conversion to a property, but the cost of the work needs to be justified by the uplift in value.

If you estimate that it will cost £1000 - £1500 per square metre plus VAT to add an extension or loft/basement conversion (without kitchen or bathroom in it) then you'll be on track to assess whether it's worth doing.

So how can you add value without adding anything I hear you ask?

Well, you do it by upgrading the internal fittings, kitchens, bathrooms, floor coverings, tiling, windows, doors, décor, and reconfiguring the existing space to make it fit what people want.

In the early days, we simply took houses and made them more appealing. Nowadays we are looking for properties where we can convert the garage or reconfigure the internal space to accommodate the current trend for open plan living.

A garage conversion is a great way to make use of what is otherwise a dead space in a home. Garages are rarely big enough to contain a modern-day car, so people tend to use them to store bicycles that they rarely use and golf clubs that get an outing even less often.

These sporting goods then get joined by miscellaneous items which really should be taken to the recycling centre, put on an auction site, or donated to charity; but we as humans get an attachment to items because of what we paid for it when we wanted it, rather than judging its actual usefulness and relevance to our present needs. If you don't use it in a year, then is it really needed in the garage? Could you do without the garage and instead have a shed to store the useful stuff?

Most people could cope with that, especially if it means that the garage can become a den or snug to stick the teenagers in when they want to meet up with their mates or watch something different on television.

Garages that are attached to a house are perfect for converting to a habitable space under permitted development. Unless your flip property is in an area where the Local Authority has taken away permitted development rights, it is very straightforward to transform 'the junk room with the big door' into a habitable space. Doing so will add massive value in comparison to the cost and appeal to buyers.

The average garage conversion should really only cost between £4,000–£6,000 – definitely the lesser end of the scale if there are no gas or electricity meters to move and if there is already a privacy door between the garage and main house.

The conversion can be done using a Building Notice, and the council will mainly be interested in insulation and means of escape. If you are replacing the garage door with a low wall and window, then provided that the window openings meet the minimum opening size requirement and have the right glass depending on the height of the window sill, then that will be pretty straight forward.

Insulation, boarding and plastering will be done by a builder who has done it before – remember to get three quotes and a recommendation from someone who has had one done recently and locally by the same company.

The electrical work will be done by a qualified electrician and this will be signed off separately to the building notice by the electrician. You send a copy of their certificate to Building Control as part of the certification process by the council.

If a new doorway is being knocked between the house and garage, then Building Control will want to check that the right lintels have been used with the right amount of overlap on the piers. Once this has all been completed it will truly transform the house and the available space which is ideal for modern-day living.

A competent builder will know the Building Control requirements and work with the inspector that comes out, so you don't need to be clued up yourself. If it is an area that interests you though, you can read up on the Approved Documents at:

https://www.planningportal.co.uk/info/200135/approved_documents.

As the economy changes and people go to pubs less and entertain at home more, their needs and desires change.

We also find that the people who buy our properties are in the age group with children or prefer to entertain at home rather than go out clubbing.

The target market for family-sized homes is very different to the target market for 1-bed flats in city centres.

People want to have a space where they can see what their children (and maybe spouse) are looking at on the internet rather than packing them off into a different room.

The kitchen has now become the heart of the home, so we try to create spaces that accommodate more than the cooker and kitchen sink.

All activity generally gravitates around the kitchen, so it is one of the most important rooms to consider when renovating or refurbishing a property for resale. This is the room that can literally make or break a sale.

In recent years, we have moved many kitchens to the rear of properties, sometimes knocking through a kitchen and dining area into one large entertaining space.

Encouraging as much light and the perception of space into the room is key. If you can achieve this by bringing the outside-in, and the inside-out, then this is ideal. If this is not possible, or if the front of the house has a preferable outlook, then this too is good. Under permitted development it is even more viable to play with the layout of a property.

There are some quite stunning examples of properties where people have added a side and rear extension to good effect. The alternative is to convert the garage and extend at the rear to create an open-plan space. If this is something you are considering doing, then it is well worth instructing an architect to give ideas to maximise the space.

The finish of the kitchen will also help to add to the feeling of light and space. Sometimes, properties can still feel small when there has been a conversion or extension because of the low ceiling height. Sometimes Building Control may demand additional insulation and this can cause the ceiling height to be reduced to 2m. This is considerably lower than the standard 2.4m that you typically get in a habitable room. Using spotlights and/or a skylight or lantern design can really improve an area and doesn't need to cost the earth. A top tip is to find a glass company to supply the glass and frames and then get your carpenter to put them together onsite. Building Control can sign off this work as standard and this can bring your cost down considerably.

The type, style and quantity of units in a kitchen can make a huge difference to the valuation of a property. Crazy, isn't it really, that the type of laminate on the front of a chipboard cupboard can affect the perceived value of a kitchen. But it does.

Since the introduction of the internet, consumers have become more discerning and spend longer deciding exactly what they want. The phrase '*keeping up with the Jones',*' was realistic in the 1930's because people only related to the Jones' that they knew or had heard about. People could only dream about the fixtures and fittings in a celebrity's house because in reality, unless a journalist or photographer was invited into their homes, you wouldn't get to see what it was like. Nowadays, people are sharing photos of their shiny new toys and fixtures and fittings. Plus, if they're not sharing this, all it takes is a journalist with a telephoto lens camera, and suddenly the images are all over the internet.

If it's not the paparazzi, then their friends are more than likely taking pics to put on social media such as Instagram, when they get invited over for parties. If you want to make a decision about the décor of your home, you are probably just as likely nowadays to make a mood board from other people's pictures on image sharing apps as you are to go to the DIY store to get a branded colour chart.

The development of the internet and the prevalence of photo sharing apps is both a good thing and a challenge for consumers. It gives the opportunity to see what everyone else thinks is good, but this can also be infiltrated into their psyche to make them think that something is a great idea, when it might actually be short lived.

If you're going to spend money on a major ticket item, make sure that it's something that is popular and photographs well. The images that go on *rightmove.co.uk* are, for some people, more important than the actual room write ups with dimensions. Your 15sqm kitchen could be 3sqm smaller than a comparable down the road, but if your finish is better, then people will be just as likely to buy yours. People buy on emotion and rationalise it afterwards, rather than the other way around.

Another trend with the current economy is that people are living with their parents longer, so it is perfectly feasible that people may be looking to move into a larger house with the future in mind.

According to the Office of National Statistics, in 2017, 26% of 20–34-year olds (nearly 3.4 million people) still lived with their parents.

People move for all sorts of reasons including:

Relocation: People relocate all the time. Workers get posted to different areas and people move for personal reasons. Where industry closes down, people are forced to move for work in order to look for more opportunity. The same is true of people as they make progress in their career. It is pretty common nowadays for people to have an hour commute from where they live to their desk and higher wages in the cities make it worthwhile.

There has to be a balance though so you'll often find people moving out of the city into more space, but still working there. People also move to be closer or further away from family. When couples have children, it is not uncommon for them to move closer to their parents so that they have more support from the extended family, when they are returning to work.

Location: People's first property may not be where they want to live, it may have been where they could afford at the time. As they become more successful in life and have access to more money, they can afford to move to better, nicer locations.

Bigger house: Having children or adding to the family can mean people want or need more space. Also, as people earn more money in their careers, they have aspirations of a bigger home as a status symbol or to have more functionality in their living space.

People looking for bigger homes because they are an established family unit will be looking for multiple bedrooms, at least two bathrooms and an ensuite to the master bedroom where possible. A set-up with multiple rooms to accommodate teens and young adults is preferable and this is where garage and loft conversions come in. If you can end up with a kitchen diner, lounge, den/snug plus two bathrooms and at least three bedrooms, then you will be onto a winner in the right location.

Outside you want to have a decent sized garden which is easy to maintain with lots of storage, so it's worth going the extra mile and getting a big shed, especially if you have converted the garage.

Parking for multiple cars will also be on their property shopping list, so bear this in mind if deciding between the pros and cons of two properties to flip. If you can do both deals great, but if you can only do one at a time, make sure you make your decision based on the end purchaser.

There is a trend in the UK of 'moving up the ladder', even if people don't need more space, so there will always be people to buy your flips, from the smallest flat to the largest mansion.

Family split: It's a sad fact but 42% of marriages end in divorce in the UK. When they do, another property is needed by at least one of the couple. If there are children, then it is likely that the new purchase will involve a family sized home in order to accommodate the children at both addresses.

Downsizing: Your flip may even be a smaller property than the purchaser's previous one. They may be releasing equity from a much larger home which they shared with children, but have since moved out, so don't assume that big is best.

It's all a numbers game and provided that the numbers result in the amount of profit you want, every size and type of property can work as a flip.

People who are downsizing tend to do so because the children have flown the nest. It is unlikely that someone would downsize further if they became bereaved because generally the amount of space you want as a single person is the same as for a couple.

People downsizing usually have more time on their hands, although they'll tell you that since they retired they are busier than they were when they worked. Nevertheless, outside space is very important.

As people get older they tend to work out how to not kill houseplants and they join the hallowed group of people who can also plant things outdoors and not kill them with the first frost of the year. This never ceases to amaze us both and we have a deep respect for people who can tend to a garden. That was a bit off topic, but it makes the point.

Nice areas to sit and entertain outside are important as is the view to the garden, so adding a conservatory or sun room to a bungalow can add great perceived value. People downsizing tend to want a separate kitchen and dining room and this is the way that most bungalows are laid out anyway, so it makes sense to keep it that way.

A large lounge to accommodate visits from family and friends is as important as a good garden. It's a good idea to fit a bath and separate shower in the main bathroom where possible as this helps with mobility issues for purchasers and their guests. It makes the property more appealing and likely to sell quicker. Off-road parking and a garage is a must have too.

First-time buyers: People are purchasing properties much later in life in the UK. This is mainly due to not being able to afford them early on and staying at home with their parents/carers or going into the rental market and possibly staying there for many years.

That said, they eventually get to the point where they are ready and able to purchase a property.

First-time buyer homes are a great place to start your property flipping journey and it's exactly where we started. The recent nil rate banding of stamp duty on the first £300k of properties with a purchase price of up to £500k bought by first time buyers is designed to help young people get on the ladder. First-time buyer houses tend to want to be modern, light, airy and functional. A great model is to focus on making terraced houses into this type of property and doing exactly the same layout changes and refurb time and time again.

Once you've found the sweet spot of buying for the right price, doing exactly the same refurb in each and commanding a good uplift in value, it is easy to systemise everything.

How to find and assess suitable flips

Looking online for properties: Now that you have decided to begin your journey as a Flipper, the first place to start looking for property is online. You should already have decided whereabouts in the country you are going to flip and also identified key 'flipzones'.

There are many websites available to search for potential properties to flip. One of the most well-known property search sites for the UK is *rightmove.co.uk*. This has been our preferred search site for the past decade. Others come and go but we still prefer this website for sourcing flips. Whatever website you choose to use, the principles are exactly the same.

You need to key in the area you are looking in. Let's use Birmingham as an example. You enter this into the search box. Then you have many options to reduce the volume of search results. You can select just that area or go out for a radius of ¼ mile to 40 miles.

You can enter the minimum & maximum purchase price. You can also specify the minimum and maximum number of bedrooms. Tick the Under Offer & STC (Subject to Contract) box to give you maximum information about an area.

In the 'property type' section initially select 'Any'. Once you get to the results page, you can apply more filters to further refine your search results. Remove the property types that are less appropriate for flips, such as the following:

- New Homes
- Shared ownership
- Over 60's / Retirement Properties

At this stage you want to be looking at all types of properties. Houses, flats, bungalows; these are all possible flips as long as they are in the right location and you can add value to them.

For your first search, leave the number of bedrooms and price range as default; that way it will show anything currently available. Then sort the order by lowest price first.

If you have picked a large area like Birmingham you will see that you have as many as eight thousand hits for your search, you may even have too many for the system to be able to show you them all. It's best if you narrow down your area into smaller flip zone areas to make sure you can get through all of the properties.

Once you have decided on your areas, you will be able to set up a search for that area with all of your criteria. That search will have the option of sending you alerts and emailing you a list of suitable properties as they become available.

You should start to do this search on a daily basis. The first time you do this will be the one which takes the most amount of time because you will be going through lots of properties. Once you have been through the whole lot and added any potentials to your list, you will be able to carry out future searches more quickly.

Once you have gone through all of the appropriate properties online, you will be able to narrow any future results down to properties added in the 24 hours, 3 days, 7 days or 14 days. This means you will very quickly be able to search on a daily basis for just a handful of properties and very quickly eliminate or add them to your list.

So now that you have a massive list of properties, what are you looking for exactly? Well, initially all you have to go on is the image, price and a small bit of text. You don't want to click on every property in the beginning as that will take you forever (although you could outsource that task). You know this is already the right area for you as that research has already been done. You now have to scan the list of properties looking at the image, price and text. Does the property look a bit dated, maybe it's so bad that the initial image showing online isn't even of the front of the property? Look for words in the description like:

- Modernisation
- Updating
- Tidy up

- Renovation
- Investment
- Tired
- Development
- Potential
- Improvement

Rightmove.co.uk now has a keyword search function where you can add up to three keywords (such as those in the above list) and sort the properties in an area by this priority. We personally think this would be better as a filter function, and maybe that change will come in the future. Zoopla.co.uk also has this additional search option.

If the house looks shiny new and the description says how amazing it is and how you can move straight in, this isn't a flip so move on.

If it shows signs from the initial image or words of being a potential flip then click on it, read the whole advert and look at all the images.

Check the location and make sure it ticks lots of the potential flip boxes. Add this to your research list and move onto the next one. It's also worth copying the URL from the search box at this stage so that you can go back to it more easily.

Repeat this process until you have gone through all of the properties. This will be daunting on the first attempt but keep going. It will be so much easier once you have gone through this first search and are only looking at a handful of properties daily.

Once you have your list of potential properties, you can do all of the online research checks using our R.E.S.E.A.R.C.H model which we will explain later.

If the agent is open, give them a call and ask any additional questions that the research couldn't uncover. If it looks promising, then organise a viewing straight away.

Get a viewing as soon as possible with no delay. If the agent can't make it for a few days or the owner needs to be contacted and you live near enough then go for a drive-by.

A lot of research can be done online, but there is always more that you can see when you are actually there. It can be quite difficult to identify the actual house on Street View as they now blank out the house numbers. You can sometimes identify it by the online image, but by physically going to the street, you should see the estate agent 'For Sale' sign and get a real feel for the road.

Once you have been doing this for a while you will really get a feel for the area. You will quickly get to know where is good and where is not so good. Do this as part of your ongoing location research process.

Online research is a big part of your property deals, so get used to the different websites and how they work, and it will soon become second nature.

You can also set up searches where you draw an area on an actual map. If your flip zones are spread out or you want to include part of an area, but other parts aren't so desirable, you can almost get down to street by street searches.

When you are out and about looking for this property, make sure you are looking at all of the others in the area too. Always have some leaflets promoting your business with you or in the car. If you see anything with potential, pop a leaflet through the door, add it in your pipeline and set up a reminder to repeat four weeks later.

Analysing a property's potential

The 8-step R.E.S.E.A.R.C.H. model

There is a lot of initial research you can do from your laptop. Each time you get a new potential flip property, get online and run through the 8-step research model. Once you've done this a few times it will become a lot easier and you will be able to do it very fast.

R = Region

You have already identified your flip zones. If the property is in one your flip zones, move onto **E**. If it looks like a good deal but is just outside the area, do some investigation to make sure that area does work as a flip zone. You need to keep revisiting your flip zones and see if things are changing in the area. This is an ongoing task. Don't be static, places are ever-changing, so keep up with what's going on.

E = Earth

The easiest way to keep up with the neighbours, or exceed them is to firstly look on Google Earth. No doubt there will be other apps that can assist you in the future, so you should keep up to date with the best free snooping applications, which at present belong to Google. Go onto Google Earth, enter the postcode of the potential flip and fly into that street from the satellite view. Have a scan of what's around that area. Try to identify which exact property on the street it is.

S = Same-street sold price comparisons

Next, we want to check out the previous sold prices. Look on the House Prices section of *rightmove.co.uk* to see what other properties in that street have sold for. On your spreadsheet, note down the date of sale, the sold price and the condition.

Sometimes you will be able to go into the original listing of the property sold, click on the image and see the condition that the property was in.

This information will remain stored on *rightmove.co.uk* long after the property has sold.

Are there internal photos online where you can see what the interior is like? Are there swirly carpets and avocado bathroom suites or does it look quite modern? Have they had a massive two-storey rear extension which means the square footage of the property is much larger?

If they have, is that something you could do to add value? Is it going to be worth it or did the bigger property only sell for £5000 more than the others? Have the other properties already had a garage conversion? Can you see a garage door? Or a loft conversion? Can you see any Velux or dormer windows in the roof space? If so, could you do the same to add value and make some chunky money? Are there floorplans that you can compare to your potential property?

All of this information is vital.

E = Extensions / Alterations

When doing your Google Earth search above, check to see which properties have been extended. Are all of the properties the same type or is there a mix?

The installed version of Google Earth will allow you to go back in time on the aerial images. Have a look to see what changes have been made and when.

If you are thinking about doing a flip and are early on in your property career, you will probably want to think about going for something that will not require planning permission.

There is a lot that you can achieve by using permitted development rights, which come under the Town and Country Planning Order 1995 and is something that can be easily researched. It is a topic that can be explored vastly, and there is a lot of detailed information which can be easily accessed.

There is a great online resource on the Planning Portal website which gives you a visual idea of what can be achieved and added to without requiring full planning permission.

That is not to say that in some projects you would not want to go for full planning permission, as you can potentially add some real value there, but if you are just starting out, sometimes the simplest option is to remodel the internal space and then look at perhaps adding a certain sized extension under permitted development without the need for a planning application.

A = Actual property research via Street View

Next go into street view mode. You can either do this directly from the listing of the property you are looking at or switch within Google Earth. Have a look at the street scene. Now it will be more obvious if all of the properties are the same type or if there is a mix. If you don't already know, you may be able to identify the actual property from the image online.

You may be able to see the door numbers (these are more commonly blurred out now), sometimes you can see the house numbers on the wheelie bins or gate posts. What can you deduce from this that would be useful to know before going on a viewing? Make a note of your findings and any questions you need ask the agent/vendor later on.

R = Research

Do some general additional research. Is the property located in a Conservation Area or does it have an Article 4 Directive? Is it a Listed Building? You should check with your local council to get a list of properties that have had permitted development rights withdrawn by the Local Planning Authority. If the property you are interested in has an Article 4 Directive, you may find, depending on the details of the Order that you can't make alterations that would otherwise have been permitted without a full planning application.

Knowing this before offering helps you to assess whether you really want to proceed with the purchase and are prepared to wait for planning to be approved. Equally, you can check to see if it is a Listed Building or locally listed online. Knowing this will help you to assess the pitfalls and the potential for profit. Visit www.historicengland.org.uk to get up to speed on The Heritage List (officially the National Heritage List for England or NHLE).

C = Ceiling price

Every street will have a ceiling price, which is the most a property of the same type and condition has ever sold for in that street. Let's say you have a street of three-bed semi-detached houses and they all look the same. You have a look on *rightmove.co.uk* and see that

Number 24 sold for £185,000 2 years ago. This was the highest recorded sold price for that street.

It is important to note that some property sold prices never make it to *rightmove.co.uk,* so there may have been some that sold for more, and equally there may have been some that sold for less. For example, some repossessed properties seemed to be missed from the records. You should keep this in mind when doing your research.

You will be able to work out the ceiling price for that street from all of the information you have already collected. If the property sales took place many years ago, prices may have gone up or down; and on some streets properties don't sell very often, so there may not be any price data available. If there are sold prices, you will already have notes of these. Workout the highest sold price for the property which is most like the one you are looking at.

Your aim with flipping is to break the ceiling price of the street, however it is important to be realistic. There is no place for ego and thinking, '*Well, mine will be better because I'm an awesome person and people will love me*'. They're not buying you, however awesome you may be. They're buying a home, so make sure that you break the ceiling price and make chunky money at the same time. Make your property better than the one that sold for £185,000. Simple!

H = Half-mile radius comparables

If there are no sold prices on that street, then you will have to look slightly further out. Depending on the area, it may be surrounded by streets of similar properties. If it is, then they are usually good comparables. However, if they are surrounded by very different properties you are going to need to find something comparable, with the same number of bedrooms, and same type of property. Then speak to three to five different estate agents to get a feel for the potential refurbished open market value.

Viewing safely

When viewing properties, your safety must be your number one priority. There are certain things that you should always have with you.

The first thing you need is a mobile phone. This is key for taking pictures and /or videos of the property whilst you are at the first viewing. If the vendor is present, then it's common courtesy to ask permission first. They are more than likely to agree if you tell them you have a rubbish memory and want to look back later when you are making decisions about the property, or you want to show someone else for reference.

This not only shows the vendor that you are interested enough to take photos, but it also helps you to work out your figures later because we guarantee that the more properties you view, the less likely you are to remember which house was which, and which one had cracks, damp or wobbly stairs.

They also come in handy when you look back at the property for planning your alterations, as by the time you complete on a purchase, the vendor will have removed their personal possessions and the property will look very different.

A torch is essential in case the power is off or you want to look in an area without lighting, such as a basement or loft. It's also likely to be pretty dark in meter cupboards, sheds and garages.

If you are viewing a property in winter in the UK, then it's more than likely that you will lose the daylight at around 4pm. Having a mobile and torch means that you can agree to meet the agent on his or her way home from the office and still get in that property as soon as they get the keys on day one.

If you are viewing a property in the evening with an agent, or going direct to vendor, then it is essential that you tell someone else where you are going and what time you expect to be finished. Get them to telephone you at this time.

As extreme as it is, you should also devise a code word. One that we use, and have never had to use is, '*Can you just check the red book to see what time I'm free tomorrow*'. This is code to tell the person you have nominated as your responsible adult that there is an issue at the property and to call the police.

Some of us are old enough the remember the disappearance of Suzy Lamplugh in 1986. Suzy was an estate agent in London who had scheduled a viewing with a 'Mr Kipper'. She disappeared and although an alleged perpetrator has made references to where she may be buried through third parties, her body has never been found and no one has been charged with her murder. This information is not designed to put you off working alone, it just serves as a reminder that your safety should be your priority.

With that in mind, it's a good idea to keep a pair of sturdy boots in the car. Not so that you can kick someone, although that's not a bad idea, but instead so that you can view the whole property including the garden.

Gardens at run-down properties are often overgrown and can harbor things such as ponds and patios to trip over. Stiletto heels are not always appropriate, so just have a think about your footwear if you're going to view an older or empty property.

Wet wipes are also an essential item as, more often than not, you will put your hand on a door knob or handrail on the stairs and find that it's not as clean as your own home.

The life of a property investor is not always glamourous and looking after your own hygiene and health is as important as keeping your sanity by photographing the properties you visit.

You might also want to carry a ladder so that you can look in the loft. DIY stores now sell telescopic ladders for around £50, so they'll fit in the boot of your vehicle for those occasions when you think a loft conversion might be possible and need to have a look.

In all of the properties we have flipped, not once has there been a loft ladder. In some properties there hasn't even been a loft hatch!

Eight common mistakes to avoid

It is easy to get carried away when you think you've found a good deal but without sounding like a killjoy, you have to remember to reign it in until you've done your due diligence. Here are some of the things you should avoid:

1. Emotional attachment: It's easy, especially if this is your first flip, to overthink the refurb and the finish of the property. You are not going to be living there.

Although you may love pink carpets and an orange bathroom suite, this is not mainstream and will put buyers off purchasing the property.

Think of each flip as stock. You buy something, you add value following a proven system and then you sell it.

It is not for you to live in, so make neutral colours your best friends and get over it. It's worth saying again, *it is not for you and you will not be living there*, so don't be tempted to jazz up the property with your own quirks, unless you are an interior designer and know what you're doing.

2. Unlawful and/or sub-standard works: Alterations to residential property in the UK must be done in accordance with the correct Planning Permission and Building Control regulations.

Using competent builders will help ensure that the works you carry out are done correctly. The Building Control department at your council will only give you sign-off if works have been carried out with due care and attention.

Sometimes you will come across a property with flip potential and you will notice that some works have already been carried out by a previous owner.

If you are purchasing a property which has had a loft conversion, garage conversion or extension, make sure that you ask for the appropriate documentation to support that it was all done correctly and get warranties to cover you too.

Loft conversions are a prime example of works that can sometimes be sub-standard to the untrained eye. We once viewed a property where the owner had literally cut a hole in the ceiling, added a ladder for access, boarded out the loft and cut away some of those 'in the way' struts.

Those struts prevent the rafters and purlins from collapsing in on themselves under the weight of the tiles in houses constructed pre-

1965 and removal should only be done under the instruction of a structural surveyor and by a competent builder.

Always ask for certification of lawful development or get a builder to check it out with you when you consider buying a property which had loft, garage or basement converted from what was originally there, especially for older properties.

There is no shortcut for undertaking structural alterations. Either do it correctly, or don't do it at all. Surprisingly this loft was advertised as an additional bedroom.

Just because the agent advertises something as a habitable room doesn't mean that you should always take their word for it.

This is a common disclaimer you will see:

"All descriptions in this brochure are the opinions of X Estate Agents and their employees with any additional information advised by the seller. Properties must be viewed in order to come to your own conclusions and decisions. Although every effort is made to ensure measurements are correct, please check all dimensions and shapes before making any purchases or decisions reliant upon them. Please note that any services, appliances or heating systems have not been tested by X Estate Agents and no warranty can be given or implied as to their working order."

The small print in an estate agent's brochure indemnifies them against mistakes, so make sure that you and your solicitor check this out before making a purchase.

3. New developments 'coming soon': Picture the scene - you purchase a lovely property for a discounted price overlooking a beautiful field in the countryside.

Your plan is to refurbish it and add a nice conservatory to show off the amazing views.

Just as you're about to market the property, you notice diggers and hoardings going up around the field. A development of 30 houses is about to start and your flip could now be worth a lot less! And it could put of your potential buyers and delay your sale.

This can be avoided though, so don't worry. With proper research and investigation prior to purchase you will avoid this issue. If you are purchasing in this type of location, your solicitor should do searches with the local authority to highlight any planning applications in the vicinity of your intended purchase.

This doesn't prevent the neighbours from submitting a planning application the day after you buy the flip, so it pays to have a think about the potential changes that others might make to an area and check that it doesn't impinge on your plans. You can also have a look at the planning portal (*www.gov.uk/search-register-planning-decisions*) and see what's happening in the area on a larger scale.

We once bought a property and the day after completion the neighbour, who we had bought the property from as a probate, put in for planning permission to build a garage at the end of the lane next to his property.

We knew that they would probably do this from the size of the plot and didn't have any objection though because what he really wanted was to build a garage, leave it there for 10 years and then get change of use to a bungalow after the prescribed amount of time had lapsed.

Our intention was to pipeline it and see if he wanted to sell the garage with planning after a few years so that we could come back and do the change of use later. So it pays to keep on side with the neighbours.

4. Flood zones: Scenic rivers are lovely, and you may well view a property in the height of summer and everything looks amazing.

If your property is situated in an area that regularly floods, it may cause a problem when you come to sell it. Insurance could be really expensive or impossible to get.

Over the past decade flooding has increasingly worsened in some areas of the UK, so if you are located in one, pay particular attention to flooding when choosing a property to flip. Most winters we see news reports of properties under water and the devastation that this causes to families.

If you are purchasing with bank finance, this should be highlighted to you by your solicitor, however you should always check yourself. You can easily do this online through your local council website using their Flood Risk Indicator. They will have information on flood areas which can usually be found in the planning section of their website.

Another resource is *www.eservices.landregistry.gov.uk*. When you buy the title deeds for a property you can also buy its Flood Risk information for about £6, although this is not always up to date or accurate. The Environment Agency is another good resource. Visit *https://flood-map-for-planning.service.gov.uk/* to assess an area.

5. Jumping in too fast: As we've already said, just because you can buy something that is cheap, it doesn't mean you always should.

Some deals look amazing and if you have yours or a JV partner's cash burning a hole in your pocket, you could be tempted to jump in too fast.

Bypassing the due diligence phase and purchasing a property without doing all of the necessary research could result in you having an unforeseen issue and ending up with a 'flip flop'. You can easily avoid this by having a documented checklist of tasks that must be done prior to purchase.

Yes, you need to act fast in some situations, but there is no substitute for due diligence.

Don't cut corners or you could lose unnecessary money. One dud deal can put you off flipping for life which would be a real shame and is completely avoidable. A simple tick list of tasks to research will mean you get the right property fast every time to get you to that chunky money.

6. Not having the right insurance: If you purchase a property with bank lending, the solicitor acting for the lender will ask for proof of insurance before they release the funds. It's really easy to get insurance for empty or flip properties and it doesn't cost much more than a standard insurance.

However, if you use cash to purchase then no one (except your investor if they are shrewd) will ask for proof of insurance. This doesn't mean it's something you should overlook to save you a few hundred quid.

You are buying an expensive asset and if things go wrong it will be your responsibility to put them right, especially if you are using other people's money. Can you afford to front up the £150,000 rebuild cost if the property is destroyed by fire? Probably not, so get insurance every time.

7. "I'll just re-paint it and put it back on the market for £30k more": If you find a property which just needs a lick of paint this is NOT always a flip opportunity. This is a property that someone on a tighter budget can buy, move into and add some new paint as they go along.

If you can easily move into the property, then it's not bad enough for you to be able to add enough value to make some real profit. It's easy to make a few thousand pounds on a property – however that's just another JOB. You're not being a property investor, you are just exchanging your time for money. You need to be able to add real value and usually everything will need to be replaced.

8.Buying in the wrong area: Scarily, "*It looks like a great deal, yes the area may be a bit run down, but someone told me that one sold once for £50k more, it's really cheap, I could turn it round very fast, surely it's a deal*" is what some new property investors think, but it's never a good strategy.

Think about your end buyer. Can they afford to buy or are they actually in rented properties? Don't forget that you are creating a product to sell. You need demand from buyers and they need to be able to get the funding to purchase. Don't do it as there are better deals out there for you.

Get rich quick doesn't exist, so stop looking for it and start getting rich the right way.

What to look for when viewing properties

One of your early priorities needs to be to get great at viewings. You want to get to the stage where you can walk into a property and know exactly what you would do with it. Experience will mean that you have an initial idea of cost of works and are able to offer there and then with the estate agent or vendor. You want to get to the point where you are confident in doing this assessment every time.

If you are new to property, then you may want to take along a friendly builder to build your confidence in what you are looking for.

A friendly builder is someone who will come with you to the property to give their opinion and give you an idea of costs, with the probability of getting the work if you secure the deal and they can hit your budgetary requirements.

Eventually you should be able to get to the stage where you know most of what you are looking for and only get a builder in for things you are unsure about. If that's something you are not at all interested in, then leverage this out as early as you can to someone who is observant and great at viewings.

This initial viewing will allow you to make a quick assessment to see whether you can add value and to list all of the changes required for that to happen. You can visit *www.tashaandkaren.com/fi-*

resources to download our viewing checklist but in the meantime, here are some things to look out for:

External aspect: What does the property look like from the front? How can you add kerb appeal? Is it a painted property, brick or other? Does it have a driveway for off-road parking; if not could you add one? Have a look down the road to see if anyone else has done this already. As long as it's not near a turning, roundabout, or a school then that should be ok in most areas, although some councils have restrictions, so you'll need to check with them to be sure.

Make a note on your spreadsheet and write down what needs to be done. Would adding a simple wooden porch over the front door make it more appealing? How much landscaping is needed?

Back garden: Are there any large trees which may cause an issue? Do any fences need replacing? Can you add a deck to tidy up an ugly concrete area? Is it overgrown?

External windows and doors: Are the windows made of UPVC and are they double glazed? Has the rubber around the glass failed or are any of the sealed units cracked and need replacing? If the windows aren't 'as new', then add them onto the 'get replaced' list. Have a look above the windows and doors. Have they previously been replaced? Is there an appropriate lintel above them?

There is nothing worse than grubby old windows, especially if you have gone to the time and effort of renovating the rest of the property. It can sometimes be an after-thought, especially if the property already has uPVC double glazing, but it is definitely something you should check when viewing a potential flip. Open all the windows and be sure to check that they open and close correctly and aren't full of black sludge. If they look new and you can clean them up, they are worth salvaging; but if there is any doubt in your mind about the perception that a buyer will have, you should upgrade them.

It is typical when replacing all of the external doors and windows in a property to pay on average £200–£300 for a fully fitted window, and £400–£600 for a regular white uPVC door. If you want to go for a coloured composite uPVC door then it will cost a bit more – roughly £800–£1000 at the time of writing, but in most cases, it will really lift the look of the property and is well worth the initial outlay. We particularly like to use black doors with a silver letterbox, handle and door knocker.

There are economies of scale to be had with windows and doors and when you build rapport with a local company, you can usually get further discounts and a bit of goodwill so that they work on a Saturday and slot you in between other jobs.

Roof: Walk across the street and have a good look at the roof. Are there any tiles that have slipped? Are there any obvious dips in the roof? Are there any gaps in the ridge tiles? Does the mortar look in good condition on the chimney? Does the chimney have lead around the bottom and is that in good condition? Write down everything you notice.

Solar panels: You would think that a property to flip would not have solar panels, but occasionally they do. Be careful when you purchase one of these that the solar panel company doesn't rent the roof from the owner, otherwise this will pass on to you and it may make it harder to sell.

We once came across a property where the owner had purchased the solar panels outright, however there was a clause in the sales pack that after selling the property the previous owner was still entitled to the income from the solar panels…. forever! Cheeky really, and he was going to struggle to sell with that clause in place, so just watch out for the small print.

Your solicitor will look through all of this whilst the purchase is going through and will let you know if there is anything unusual; but it's better to know from the outset before you make an offer.

External Brickwork: Are there any obvious cracks in the property? How big are they? Are they aesthetic issues, serviceability issues or stability issues and do you know the difference? Do they follow the mortar line or do they go straight through a brick? How many cracks are there? This can be indicative of a significant issue that you may not want to tackle, unless you are an experienced trader.

Flat roofs: If the property has a flat roof section, have a look at it from an upstairs window. You should be able to see the condition of a flat roof. What is it made of? How much life is left in it?

Surrounding area: Take a look from the upstairs windows to see what's happening around the property. Is there any sign of building work in empty fields? Are there any really large trees near the property which may cause a problem? This is also a good time to see if you can spot any of the neighbouring houses that have had any extensions added to the property which may explain a higher price.

Internal condition: It is very likely that you will need to replace everything in a flip. Make sure you have a good look around and make a physical note of everything.

In each room, note where the radiators are and their condition. Where is the boiler located and what model is it? Quite often in these properties there will be a back boiler behind an old fireplace.

Whatever the fuel source, the boiler is something that will probably benefit from upgrading to a combi, unless it has been installed in the last few years and serviced regularly.

When upgrading a heating system, you should look not only at the boiler, but also at the condition of the radiators to see if they look modern and efficient. There are two ways you can make existing ones more appealing if you're not doing a full replacement.

The first way is to give them a good clean, that's after you have pulled out all of the sweet papers and fluff from behind them, and then paint them white with radiator paint.

The second way is to replace all of the Thermostatic Radiator Valves (TRVs) when you replace the boiler and the system is drained down. This will give them a little aesthetic lift and will renew the lifespan of the radiator.

The third solution is to replace the whole system including the radiators. We pay about £3,500 - £4,500 on average for a full replacement in a three-bed house.

If you come across a property which has a microbore system (tiny copper pipes), then in our experience it is more expensive (because of the labour element) to try and fault find and fix the system than it is to replace it and start again.

If you can manage to keep hold of the copper and take it to a metal recycling centre, then you'll make some of your money back. At approximately £2.60-£3.60/kg, you stand to make some decent money. If you have a copper immersion tank, then that alone is worth

£40 to you at the scrapyard. This is why they always disappear first when plumbers get on site.

When you take your copper tanks to the scrapyard, don't be offended if they cut them to check you haven't tipped a bit of concrete in! Scrapyards work on weight, so separating out different types is especially important for more valuable metals such as copper, brass, lead, stainless steel and cable. Old metal beds and radiators are classed as light iron and will just be done on the weighbridge as you drive in and out. You'll need to register at:

www.gov.uk/waste-carrier-or-broker-registration to transport your waste and take proof of ID to the scrapyard. They'll then pay you either into a debit account or by cheque so that the transaction is traceable.

Have a look at the light switches, are these modern looking? If they are brown round Bakelite-style switches, then they are very old and the whole house will need a rewire. Just make a note of this and move on.

What about the electrical sockets, are these modern? What are the ceiling lights like? Take pictures as you go to remind you when you get home. If you are viewing multiple properties, take the first picture of the street name and then the front door with the house number on it. That way you can easily remember which house is which when you go back through the camera.

Find the fuse board / consumer unit - is this the old type with the individual brown chunky pull out fuses with a little blue, red or white dot? If so, this will need to be replaced.

Look to see where the soil pipes run in the property. Typically, in an upstairs bathroom they will go straight out through the wall and down, so you will be able to spot them when you are outside the property. Make a note of their location. You will often get an upstairs bathroom above a downstairs one. This is important if you are going to add an ensuite or relocate an existing bathroom. Also remember to check the floorplan for windows & doors as these can sometime be wrong in the estate agent's plan.

General décor: This will always need updating but it's good to note how much prep work will be required. Is it plastered, wallpapered or does it have forty-seven layers of woodchip that will need to be attended to?

Internal walls: Are there any significant cracks in the walls? Is there anything obviously bowing, leaning or deformed? Do they look or smell damp? Make a note of what you have observed and exactly where it occurs.

Fireplaces: Note where existing fireplaces are, some may be boarded up, while others are still exposed. Has the downstairs section of the chimney been removed but the first floor section is still there? Is it adequately supported? You'd be surprised at what some DIYers do.

Nicotine: One of the most stubborn things to remove or cover up are ceilings covered in years and years of nicotine. Even if the ceiling looks nice and smooth, sometimes it is just easier to overboard it or replace it because by the time you have added 3 coats of anti-stain paint followed by 5 coats of emulsion, you will have wished you did (this is speaking from experience!).

Loft hatch: This is an interesting one. We once purchased a mid-terrace property that didn't even have a loft hatch. It was one of our first flips and wasn't on the early checklist so we didn't notice, that was until we wanted to insulate the roof space. It's not a problem; your builder just needs to add one correctly in the upstairs ceiling where appropriate, but worth adding onto the list.

Loft space: Always have a look into the loft. If you can't access it on the first viewing, make sure you go back and have a look. It's a great way to check out the roof, you may be able to see light coming in to identify possible slipped tiles.

Also have a look at the construction, is it possible to do a loft conversion?

Some of the old Victorian terrace properties can have loft space which isn't separated between houses! This means that you can go into your loft and basically run down the entire street along the loft space – scary. Also, with fire and safety regulations, it is best to block these up. Your builder can do this with bricks, but fireboard can be a much easier, quicker way to achieve the same thing when installed correctly.

Flooring: You will see lots of wild and wonderful carpets of all shades, colours and patterns; these will all need to be replaced.

Bathroom: Unless there is a new white suite, this will need to be completely replaced and re-tiled.

Kitchen: The kitchen is a great place to add value. Can it be re-located to make it bigger, more functional or more appealing? Remember to make a note if it's a gas or electric oven and hob so you have this information to hand in your planning phase.

Floorplans

When doing research, you need a floorplan of the property. Lots of estate agents now use 3D floorplan software. This may look pretty for some people however for traders we want the standard 2D version.

The agent should be able to give you a copy of that. If not just create your own.

It doesn't have to be perfect; you can use something as simple as graph paper if you like to work with a pencil and paper or the 'Paint' program on your windows computer.

There are also many floorplan apps available which make life easier, or you could get someone on *Fiverr.com* to do it for you from your sketches.

You will need this floorplan when you go to view a property.

Take the floorplan with you and make sure it is correct. We have found quite often that doors or windows are in the wrong place. Remember to take a note of where the soil stack (the toilet pipe) is, and where it runs from the property.

What to avoid and be aware of

When viewing or doing up a property that has laid empty for a little while, the public's activity near the property might not be as desirable as you might like.

If there is a big hedge, you'll often find that if it is on a busy road that people will just ram empty cans, beer bottles and crisp packets into it, instead of using the litter bin just down the road. This is true of all types of areas and not just lower demographic neighbourhoods.

I'll never forget the day we came to site one morning to find that overnight someone had opened the lid of the wheelie bin, hung their backside over it and defecated in the bin. The smell will haunt me forever. We put it down to it being someone on a night out or walk home, rather than a dirty protest by a neighbour. Logistically though, you'd have to be pretty tall to pull that one off or have very good balance. Needless to say, we were impressed in an unimpressed way.

On another occasion we found that same wheelie bin halfway down the street with just a pair of nude tights hanging out of it. Fortunately, the former owner of the tights wasn't in there with them, although we did check just in case it was the same person as before who hadn't been as nimble the second time around.

The bottom line is, when it comes to property refurbs, expect the unexpected and take caution where caution is needed. You will require specialist surveys and removal if you or your builder suspects asbestos might be present. If a property has a chequered history then you do need to be diligent about the safety of you and your team.

Sometimes, you might come across a property where there has been needle use and this is something to watch out for if you or your team are clearing out soft furnishings, furniture or sometimes outhouses.

We once bought a property and whilst the owner had left the property clear of all possessions, the same couldn't be said for the shed. During the clear out we came across hundreds of used hypodermic needles. It turned out that the previous resident was diabetic, however we still had to proceed with caution.

If you come across a hazard like this, then there are specialist companies who will do a 'Clean and clear' service, or you can buy sharps bins for the disposal of needles from many online retailers relatively cheaply, and these can be collected by local authorities for safe disposal.

Section 4: How to minimise risk and maximise potential

Section 4: How to minimise risk and maximise potential

It is <u>all</u> about the numbers

When starting out as a Flipper, it is a good idea to start with a smaller property to learn the trade and get everything in place to launch you to bigger projects in the future. Within your 'flipzone' area you will no doubt find a 'profit sweet-spot' price bracket.

If you buy a flip for around the £100k - £120k, do a good (but cost effective) refurb and sell; you could make £10k to £15k profit.

If you step up a little into £120k to £175k purchase price bracket, doing a higher-spec refurb, you could be looking at the £20k to £40k profit bracket. There will also be less competition from BTL investors. Doing the slightly larger, higher spec property won't actually take much longer and the effort needed for managing it is almost the same.

See the next table for the profit sweet-spot guidelines. As a Flipper you could concentrate on the middle section, make this your niche and get multiple flips going. You can apply this principle all over the country and adjust the theoretical purchase prices to the actual figures for your area.

Purchase Price	Refurb cost	Potential Profit
First time buyer properties: £100k–£120k	£10k-15k	£10k–£15k
Family homes or second step on the property ladder: £120k–£175k	£20k–£30k	£20k–£40k
Larger or detached homes £175k–£250k+	£40k+	£30k–£50k+

Working out your profit potential with our P.A.W.S. formula

As I'm sure you are very aware by now; profit is an important part of flipping property. Our P.A.W.S. formula will give you the structure to work out your potential profit.

In the following sections we will go into more detail on how to work out what everything is likely to cost. Once you have all of that information you will be able to work out the profit potential in each project.

We can't give you the actual figures, but we can tell you how to gather the information with confidence and work it out yourself.

P.A.W.S. for profit – Property flipping is a very straight forward numbers game.

$$\text{SOLD PRICE} - \begin{bmatrix}\text{Purchase price}\\ \text{Acquisition costs}\\ \text{Works}\\ \text{Selling costs}\end{bmatrix} = \text{PROFIT}$$

Everyone has a different reason 'Why'. You should have yours written down from earlier on. Flipping is all about the numbers. The reason you are looking at flipping property is because you would like to make some chunky money.

We live in a world where you need money to do almost anything, and even if your reason 'Why' is to give back, you still need cash to do that; that is just the way the world works.

It's great if you enjoy property, the journey and the process. It can be really fun, very rewarding and you can meet some amazing people along the way. But you are doing this for a much bigger reason and using it as your vehicle to achieve your reason 'Why'.

We happen to love it and really enjoy the process (well the parts we choose to do), but that's not important. You MUST know what outcome you want from each and every flip from the start. If it doesn't add up, DON'T do it. The outcome is always a number, fact.

What do you want to make from a flip? That may seem like a difficult question, but if you don't know this then you can't work out anything else.

So let's be realistic here. If you are buying a £100k house, it is very unlikely you will be able to make £500k profit. If you are buying a £2m property, then that is much more viable. Yes, we all want to make good money and fast, but be realistic with what you are buying. If this is your first flip, then maybe start with a smaller one.

There are 6 parts to the P.A.W.S formula:

1. SOLD PRICE – The amount that the property will realistically sell for once all of the works are complete.
2. **P** – PURCHASE PRICE – Simply the amount you pay to purchase the property.
3. **A** – ACQUISITION COSTS– This includes purchasing legal fees, surveys, stamp duty (SDLT) and the cost of finance.
4. **W** – WORKS– The actual cost of the works done to the property. This also includes the ongoing property bills such

as gas, electric, council tax, insurance, water and your tax when due etc.

5. **S** – SELLING COSTS– Legal costs, estate agent fees.
6. PROFIT

P.A.W.S – Purchase Price

Let's use the £100k purchase price as a starting point. Depending on your investment area, you may or may not be able to buy property for that amount, however let's just use this number as a starting point for now. What net amount do you want to make from that property? I want you to write down a number.

If you pick the right property in the right location, then £10k should be very easy. £20k should be very achievable. £30k may be possible. It all depends on the property, location, quality of finish and your buyer.

Once you know your 'chunky money profit figure', you can then work out everything else and know for sure what you should offer for the property. Without this profit figure, you can't work out anything else.

For this example, let's say you are going to purchase a property for £100k and are looking to make at least £20k profit. A good way to look at it is as a 'percentage of the purchase price'. In this example it's 20% so:

- 20% of £100k = £20k
- 20% of £200k = £40k
- 20% of £300k = £60k
- 20% of £500k = £100k
- 20% of £1M = £200k

You will need to work out what is right for you, but this is a great starting point. Would you be happy making £20k from your first flip? Would that help towards your reason 'Why'?

Now you need a plan of works to be done. You will know from your initial viewing what needs to be done and this should all be documented in your flip calculator spreadsheet. Things to consider might be: new kitchen, new bathroom, add an ensuite, decorate throughout, new carpets, flooring, windows and external doors, internal doors, garden and landscaping.

Next you need to work out the cost of the refurb. This is a part which most people are worried about. They are concerned they will be ripped off and have no idea what things cost. This feeling is totally normal as when you start something new you don't know what you don't know. That's why you are reading this book, so let us take you through this journey.

What costs do you need to consider?

You need to know your numbers and you need to make sure you have accounted for all costs in your initial evaluation of a property. You want to hit your required profit and the only way to do that is to include everything and be realistic. Don't just make the figures look good. If you choose to do that, the only person you are kidding is yourself.

We are now going to break down the numbers in the P.A.W.S. formula even further.

P.**A**.W.S = Acquisition costs, including:

- Legals
- Surveys
- Stamp Duty (SDLT)
- Lending

Legals: Once you have an offer accepted, you will need to instruct your solicitor to start the legal buying process. If you already have a good solicitor that's great. If not then look for one who is a property specialist, someone who deals with more than just residential and single buy-to-let purchases. A great way to find a good one is to ask other property investors who they use and go through recommendations. Once instructed, the solicitor will send you their agreement to sign and usually ask for a bit of cash up front to have on account. Fees will vary from deal to deal, however for this deal with a purchase price of £100k, we are estimating the solicitor fee to be roughly £1000 for a purchase by a limited company, which should include the following charges:

- The Solicitor's Fee
- Companies House registration Fee
- Telegraphic Transfer Fee
- Local Searches
- Land Registry Search
- Bankruptcy Search

Surveys: If you are getting bank lending on the property, the lender will send out a person to value to property. It's their job to make sure the property is worth at least what you are paying for it and that the lender has adequate security. You have the choice to have a basic valuation, a home buyer's survey or a structural survey. We will explain the difference in more detail later on. Cost wise, they are roughly:

Basic: £300–£450

Home Buyers: £700–£1000

Structural: £1000–£1500

If you are buying the property with cash, then you don't have to have a survey, but it's a good idea anyway if you are just starting out or find things you haven't experienced before. Alternatively, you could take an experienced builder to check out the property prior to purchasing.

Don't underestimate the value of a good surveyor. If they find a problem with the property, it may give you bargaining power and you may be able to get a reduction on the purchase price. Equally, if it's going to be a flip flop because of a structural issue that you hadn't spotted, then it'll be the best £1500 you spend.

Stamp Duty: Over time, stamp duty (SDLT) and other taxes change. At the time of writing this book, traders pay an additional rate of stamp duty compared to homeowners who only have one property. The purchase of a £100k property by a limited company would incur stamp duty of £3,000 at the time of writing. The best thing to do is search online to see what the latest stamp duty costs for your price bracket and circumstances are.

Lending: If you have borrowed the money to purchase the property from a bank or a JV partner there will be costs to add to the loan amount. With a JV partner, you will have agreed the terms and conditions already so will know these numbers. You could set the loan on a simple rolling monthly (paid at completion) amount.

If you are borrowing from a bank, make sure you include all of the costs of the loan. The lender's paperwork will list all of the costs. These may include an application fee, a bank transfer fee, setup fee and of course the interest itself. Again, project this for 12 months when working out the numbers. Don't forget to include the cancellation fee if there is one.

Next we need to understand the cost of the physical works you are intending to undertake. We also need to take into account the standard ongoing costs that you as the owner will pay.

P.A.**W**.S = Works & property bills, including: -

- All material & trade costs
- Utility bills
- Insurance
- Council tax
- Tax at your prevailing rate

Works: Once you have your complete list of jobs (schedule of works), you will be able to assess an approximate cost for these. For every job you have, make sure to always get three quotes. Once you have used tradespeople a few times and you are happy with their work and prices, you can continue to use them. Just be aware that quotes may start to creep up as you become more visible/successful.

Keeping records and occasionally getting new tradespeople in to quote will keep everything up to date and the prices keen. Prices do naturally rise over time, but so can your selling price. Just as long as the numbers stack up, and you achieve at least your projected profit, that is the important thing.

We have compiled a list of tasks that you might undertake as part of a flip. You can download this from our website (*www.tashaandkaren.com/fi-resources*).

Different parts of the country will vary in terms of labour and materials pricing. Some will be more, and some will be less.

A tool to investigate is *www.estimators-online.co.uk* which combines regional prices from builders' merchants and local trades' labour prices. It is a paid for estimating service, but well worth considering for your first flip.

P.A.W.**S** – Selling costs, including;

- Legal fees

- Estate agent's fee

Legal fees: Once you have refurbished the property and have had an offer from your buyer, let your solicitor know and they will prepare the paperwork for you. The conveyancing process can take up time so make sure to instruct the right solicitor who will work quickly and avoid any delays.

You will need to complete a number of detailed questionnaires about the property and what you intend to include with the sale. Your solicitor will then draw up a draft contract and send it to the buyers' solicitor. Once the negotiations are completed (completion date, fixtures, additional costs, etc.), solicitors will exchange contracts and set a date for completion.

Immediately after exchange, your solicitor should receive the buyer's deposit (usually 10% of the purchase price). On completion day, you hand over the keys (usually through the estate agent). After completion, you will have to pay your solicitor/conveyancer and the estate agent before receiving your profit.

Estate agent's fee: Later we will go into detail about how to instruct an agent and how to negotiate what to pay them. Add this figure into your costs spreadsheet.

The SOLD PRICE - (P-A-W-S) = PROFIT formula will tell you the potential profit you will make once you have completed the flip if everything goes to plan. If the PROFIT figure matches, or is higher than, your required PROFIT then go for it, fast.

How to negotiate like a pro

What's the most important number? Your net profit! You also need to work out your tax deduction based on your personal circumstances and factor that into the equation.

Your maximum offer needs to use the formula SOLD PRICE - (P.A.W.S) = YOUR PROFIT. If you offer over that price, then you are impacting your required profit and you need to be aware of that. Be realistic with your profit and stick to it. Don't offer your maximum price first.

When people put their properties on the market, they will usually get some valuations and often go with the highest, because they believe that if someone has valued it at this price then that's what it is worth.

You may be thinking, but if I get 3 estate agents round why do I get such different valuations? Surely a house is worth what a house is worth, right?

Well no, it's all down to the following and you should keep this section in mind both for when you are purchasing a property and for when you are putting your flip property back onto the market:

Comparisons: When doing your research and going through our 8-step R.E.S.E.A.R.C.H model, you will be looking at sold comparisons or comparables, just like the estate agents do when they value a property. It's exactly what the valuers do when working for the mortgage company and buyer. In fact, when the estate agent comes to your property they will more than likely take a print out of the local similar properties that have sold, some that are currently on the market and even some available for rent in the area. They will then let you know what they think it is worth. So why do you get three very different valuations?

Let's have a look at one of our flip properties. We went through the 8-step research model and predicted that the property would sell for about £180k and would give us our 20% of purchase price profit. We purchased the property, did the full refurb and were ready to put it back onto the market. We asked three different estate agents to come to the property to value it for sale. The three valuations were:

1. £145,000
2. £185,000
3. £215,000

But how can this be? Well, there are a number of reason for this. Firstly, it is down to individual opinion, which will always vary and is just human nature. But when you get such a wide range of valuations there must be more to it. To be fair this isn't a reflection on all estate agents, we have some great ones we work with and they are always open and honest.

If the valuation comes in really low, it may be that for some reason that estate agent doesn't really want the property. Don't take this personally as it may be that they already have lots of that type of property and are struggling to shift them.

It could be that it's actually outside of their current target area, so they will give you a low valuation to put you off going with them.

They may well put a low price because they know they will sell it tomorrow at that price and if they were lucky enough to be the only agent going around then they may well get a deal and minimise the work.

The middle valuation of £185k was realistic, they had gone through their research properly and put forward a reasonable price, they wanted the property and wanted to put in the work to sell it.

The highest valuation of £215k was by a chancer. What they were hoping for is that you see the pound signs and go with them. They may well tell you how they have 25 people on their books ready to view and an extra 10 people per week enquiring about this type of property in this location, and how they usually sell within 2 weeks and so on and so on.

These guys do win lots of instructions because everyone wants as much as they can get for their property.

Just be mindful of the reality. If you go with the highest, this is what may happen. It will hit the market, you may get a couple of viewings initially, then nothing for a few weeks. Four weeks in they call to say, "*The market is quiet so perhaps it would be best to drop the price a little to encourage more interest in the property*". They persuade you to drop to £199k.

You get a couple more viewings, but another four weeks later they say again, "*Maybe we should drop the price as all of the feedback is good about the property, but if we drop it a little more it will go below the next bracket and get loads more hits online*".

What these people are doing is getting your custom initially by showing you the money.

They will quite often try to lock you into a 16-week contract, which is more like a life sentence. During the 16-week period they will slowly drop the price enough to sell the property before the end of the term and make their commission.

You now have had the property on the market for an extra 4 to 6 months and all of the additional costs such as gas, electric, water, council tax, insurance, lending and garden maintenance.

You have also now sold the property for close to what you thought it was worth anyway and if you had gone with the more realistic valuation you would have actually saved lots of money, increasing your profit.

Also, you should make yourself aware of the estate agent's fee structures. We are all about paying a good amount to an estate agent we can work with and who can get the sale quickly (see our section on what to pay estate agents later).

Let's start with the £215k estate agent. You agree to pay the agent a 2% fee. They work out 2% of the £215k and write £4,300+VAT = £5,160 as their fee.

You will sign the paperwork and the £5,160 is then set as a fixed fee. That way they get 2% of £215k, but what if you sell the property at £185k? 2%+VAT of £185k = £4,440, but you just paid £5,160.

You can see who is winning there; they are getting a much higher % by fixing it at a higher price and they have no incentive to achieve anything higher as they get the same commission no matter what!

The way to ensure this doesn't happen is to make sure they put 2% (or whatever % you agree) of sale price in the documentation - there is a box for this and they should use it. This then incentivises them to negotiate a higher offer from the buyer.

You can see how some property owners you are buying from may have some unrealistic ideas of value and that could just be down to the agents they use.

Now, going back to making an offer. With run-down flip properties, they may already be empty, they may be a probate property where the remaining family live far away, or it may be a distant relative who has no emotional attachment to the property. It's a good idea to know the situation of the sale, who is selling it, why is it being sold and who makes the final decision on the sale price. This will give you much more negotiating power.

Let's say that someone does still live there, and they do have an attachment to the property. You need to be a bit more careful with the offers you make in this instance.

We sometimes need to make a low offer as the property is just too expensive in the current market to enable you to achieve your profit.

Also you never want your first offer to be your maximum otherwise you have nowhere to go from there. You want the seller to feel like they have won and they have pushed you to the top price you can pay.

Generally, I would suggest you have 3 offers, maximum, to play with. If you have a great relationship with the estate agent, then this becomes much easier to achieve. Make sure you are building those relationships, although you won't get that with every agent.

Find out how many viewings there have been, ask if any offers have been received and if any were anywhere near the asking price.

The agent isn't allowed to tell you what the offers are, but you can get a general idea. Tell the agent all of the concerns you have with the property and if your numbers aren't very close to the asking price; explain that the property just doesn't work for you at that price.

List the issues and costs involved to fix them, then say that you can't make an offer on that property as the numbers don't stack up, it would need to be £X amount for it to work for you.

Pause to see what the response is. This way you are offering without offering. The agent will either say, "*So it that an offer?*", which the answer to is "*Yes*", or they will say *"It's too low"*.

Now, from here you can play the waiting game, however if there is a high demand in the area you may miss out. Or you could say, "*Realistically it is a high price for the condition of the property. What do you think they would take?*" This may push them to an answer. Either way, add the details into your pipeline spreadsheet and set a date to follow up.

How to finance your flips

Flipping property will give you chunky money which in turn gives you the freedom and choice to do the things you want, whenever you want. Let's be honest, none of us are in it for the money alone because money alone is meaningless. It's the things that money gives you – freedom, choice, stability and certainty - that makes it attractive.

We remember posting a few things on social media around the time that we started our property journey and the little rewards we gave ourselves which attracted a response, from someone who we are still friends with, that just read:

"God help you the day you don't have any money'"

I (Karen) remember thinking; 'You have no idea how hard we've grafted'.

It doesn't matter that he doesn't know what that comment would actually mean to me. He was living in a house-share in London. His rent alone was probably £850 a month which is a massive amount and leaves very little surplus to enjoy being in your twenties. What he doesn't know is that I do have experience of having no money; and that we value everything that we have achieved and everyone who is in our lives.

When I was at university, I experienced having no money. And not in the regular sense of being a poor student having blown the student loan on beer and baggy jeans, because I hadn't.

I literally had zero money during one summer break between semesters at University because I'd taken a job in London to work in a B2B call centre. Although I was due to earn £15/h, it costs a lot to just get there, get the job through an agency and get the train every day.

The first pay cheque was a few days away, but I headed out to find some lunch and found the cheapest thing I could – a sad cheese sandwich in a newsagent for £1. I asked the shop keeper if he would take a cheque. He looked at me with disbelief in his eyes. "It's just £1" he said. "Yes", I said, "But I don't have £1 until Friday". And with that I left the shop empty handed and embarrassed.

That night I thought about how to get some food and decided that I didn't want to go through the embarrassment at the supermarket of trying to pay by cheque in case they said I could use the cheque card instead.

I then realised that the minimum spend at the Chinese takeaway was £10 if you wanted to pay by cheque. So that's what I did. My conscience let me, because I knew that by the time the cheque cleared, I would have received my first pay packet. I would also have less left because of the way I had to spend in order to eat that week.

So, you see I know exactly what it feels like to have no money. And (although my experience was very short-lived) I know the struggles that you go through in that situation and where it leaves you if you have no exit route.

I quickly realised that things had to change, and I vowed after that experience to never leave myself so vulnerable again when it comes to money. After all, it was just £1, but £1 is no different to £100,000 if you can't think of a way to get it.

So with that in mind, let's talk about how to get the money to do your flips.

Abundance mindset: People come into money all of the time. If you believe that you'll find someone to fund your deals, if that's what you need, then you will find the money. But you have to actively look for it, not just chant or visualise. Chanting, meditation and visualisation techniques are great for personal wellbeing and getting balance. However, in order to get some action, you have to act.

The potential will always be there, but you need to believe that you can do it and then take action in order to get some results as illustrated below.

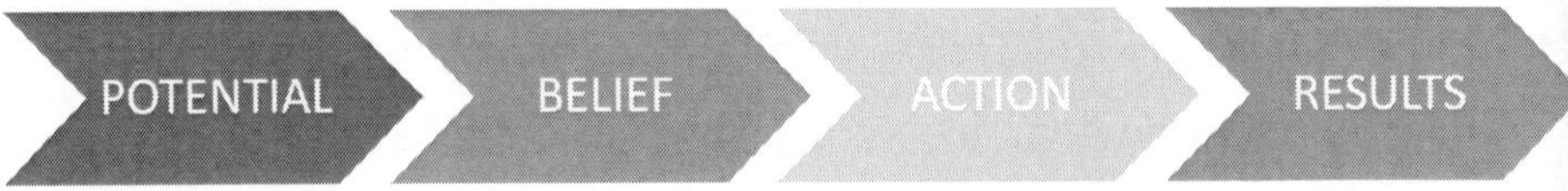

Here are some ways in which people may come into surplus money:

- Inheritance
- Pension (retirement age)
- Pension release – SIPP or SSAS
- Management buy-out of business
- Lottery win
- Divorce
- Re-mortgage
- House sale
- Scratch card
- Gift from a relative
- Redundancy money
- Bonus from work
- Insurance pay out
- Payment Protection Insurance (PPI)
- Sickness on holiday pay-out (yes, this is a real thing!)
- Negligence pay-out

- Maturing bonds
- ISA cash
- Premium bonds
- Archaeological find
- Realisation of assets – i.e. selling the family jewels at the antiques roadshow

The money is there and with billions, trillions, and even quadrillions of dollars in the world, you have to ask yourself why you don't yet have more of it.

Imagine for a second that you borrow £100k from a private financer in order to do your first flip. You make £25k net profit and after you've paid that person back you have £20k profit to put down as a deposit on a single let, maybe even two in the North East. You can still go back to that financer and see if they want to loan again on another flip. The chances are, they'll ask you if they can loan to you before you ask them because you are making them £5k a year for doing very little.

As we write, the Bank of England has raised base rate back up to 0.50% from the 0.25% that it had been at for a couple of years.

The impact of the current interest rate means that a saver with £10,000 in an easy access account, will now receive 0.65% pa or £65 a year!

We typically pay our lenders 0.5% a month (6% pa), so on £100k loan an investor would stand to make £6,000 a year (minus tax at their prevailing rate), instead of £650 that they would get in the bank.

Starting a conversation about joint ventures is very easy when armed with that information. Ask yourself, if you had £100k spare, would you rather make £650 in the bank, or £6,000 from doing very little this year? The answer, when coupled with credibility and confidence is always the latter. In fact, some of our investors choose to leave their money with us for multiple years and earn year on year compounding interest meaning that they make a lot more money than they ever would in a bank.

Joint Ventures: A Joint Venture (JV) starts out as just a blank piece of paper. The important thing is to get to know your JV partner and find out what they are looking for in a JV with you. You can then begin to draft a Head of Terms to send to your solicitor for them to draw up a contract for you both.

You need to be clear about the return you are going to pay and the term of the loan. We find that one of the most important meetings is the one where you discuss all of the 'what if' questions. This is so important because it helps to clear up any uncertainty moving forward.

For example, let's say you find a private financer who has £100k to loan. You get to know them and find you can work to together. You agreed a 6% return over a fixed term of 12 months. The likelihood of the project taking exactly 12 months is very small. This is where you need to decide on the structure. What if the project finishes at 6 months? (this is what you are aiming for). What if it goes over 12 months? Setting a definite term is difficult in a flip scenario because it sells when it sells, and that exact date can't be predicted.

The JV partner or private financer will understand the process as you will have taken them through it, so how about agreeing a monthly % return and a term which follows the flip. For example, 0.5% per calendar month until sale of the property – the cash invested plus interest to be paid when property sells.

Another 'what if' question we get is "*What if you die*?" It's a perfectly normal question to ask, a bit ahead of time maybe, but actually quite telling – it could mean that the investor is thinking about the long term rather than day to day. Depending on the security the investor wants there will be legal documents which show their interest in a particular property, the amount invested and the return.

Their money is secured on a property, so if you were to die, it would go to probate and the money would be paid back as part of the probate process.

Joint venture security: Your JV partner will more than likely want some kind of security on their investment. There are many different levels of security to choose from including the following:

1. **Verbal agreement or a handshake**

As unlikely as it may sound if you are new to joint ventures, some people will invest or borrow large quantities of money without any formal written agreement. It's just the way that some people operate and the longer you are in the business, the more likely you are to come across people who do business this way.

Be assured that there is still a level of protection afforded to each party. This is because English law makes provision for a contract to be implied if terms and conditions have been agreed, either face-to-face, via telephone, text, email or even Facebook for a service.

2. **Partnership agreement**

A partnership agreement is a written document which sets out the agreed terms and conditions you discuss with your JV partner. You both have a copy which you sign and get independently witnessed.

If you are entering into a verbal agreement, it is likely that you will just take that extra step and write down what has been agreed. You file it with your last will and testament or other important papers.

This doesn't generally involve a solicitor and it's the least formal type of agreement in terms of having a professional check it over, but it is still a legally binding document and would stand up in an English court of law if terms and conditions have been agreed. This would typically be used with family or friends where you already have that trust in place by knowing them for a long time.

Some JV partners that you work with for many years may also be happy with this after a few deals with you. The partnership agreement can have a property mentioned in it to show where the money is, however there are no legal charges or restrictions placed on the property.

3. Deed of Trust with restriction

A Deed of Trust is the document which accompanies a restriction being placed on a property. To form a Deed of Trust, you start with a blank piece of paper and draft a Heads of Terms together. It will contain the name and address details of you and the other party, the amount borrowed and the term of the loan.

A solicitor will then use this information to insert into an industry standard template which also contains the 'what if' clauses. Once you have done this once, you will have a template to use in future with joint ventures, but a solicitor will still need to look over and independently review it.

A restriction can be placed on any property as security either with or without the legal owner's permission. If choosing this level of security, then it is being done with your knowledge and permission so you would obviously agree to the restriction. It is worth knowing that you can place a restriction on any property where you can demonstrate that the owner owes money or you have a genuine interest in the property.

Most people don't realise this when they break up with a partner after a few years of living together and were jointly contributing to the cost of a property. Even if it is legally only owned by one person you can still place a restriction if you contributed towards the deposit etc.

A restriction will be done by you or your solicitor using a RX1 form. It provides information to solicitors acting for the property owner to tell them who else has an interest in the property, and what amount or proportion of the profits they are owed if the property is sold or re-financed.

The restriction will also appear on the title deeds which can be bought by anyone from *www.eservices.landregistry.gov.uk*, but won't always indicate the amount that is owed to the lender. The same is true of a mortgage lender. It'll tell you who is owed money by way of charge in the charges register, but not the financial amount.

4. Second charge

A second charge can be placed on a property to secure the JV money. If you have additional lending in the form of bank lending or pension fund for example, then they will always want a first charge against the property. Some banks are happy for there to be a second charge too, just check with your broker and make sure that you declare it. A second charge is done by your solicitor. When the property is sold the first charge owed to the bank or other institutional lender is always paid off first, and then the second charge can be paid to your investor.

5. First charge

A first charge can only be made once per property and as already explained, will be required by any commercial lender. However, if your JV partner is putting in all of the cash and you don't need any additional lending, you can offer a first charge to your JV partner if it is important to them. This will be done by your solicitor and will be written into the legal documentation, so when the property is sold the person or entity who holds the first charge will always get paid back first.

Bank finance: Ok, so you have found a great property in a great location which has potential to refurb and add value. You have gone through the 8-step research formula, you know your profit figure and you have had an offer accepted. If you have the deposit money yourself, or don't want/require a private financer then you can apply to a financial institution for loan. There are two different types of bank loans, both of which have varying terms and conditions, so you'll benefit from using a qualified broker to help you navigate which is the best deal for your flip:

1. **Bridging**

Bridging finance works well for flips as it's a short-term lend. Because of this the interest rates are usually higher, but you can get deals with no exit fees. It's great to have a flexible end date with flips as you don't know exactly when it will sell.

2. **Commercial finance / Development loan**

You will need a good broker to help you identify the best commercial or development finance for you. You can also approach some banks directly and get a meeting with the Relationship Manager. You will need to meet certain lending criteria and demonstrate that you will be making a big enough annual turnover to be seen by the Relationship Manager. Having a portfolio of properties when you do this shows credibility and that it's not just a hobby.

Some banks will lend on a roll-up basis. They'll lend you a proportion of the purchase and refurb costs and estimate a predicted end valuation before you start based on the schedule of works you supply and the sold comparables in the area. You then accrue the monthly repayments and roll them into one final settlement when the project ends. Other banks will have products where you make a repayment on a monthly basis, much the same as a mortgage. But the products will be short term and specifically for projects that you intend to sell.

Vendor Finance/ Assisted Sale: If you get the deal directly through the owner of the property you may be able to do an assisted-sale deal. How it works is that you agree a purchase price with the owner, for ease of numbers let's say it's £90,000, but you don't buy it outright. You then fund and carry out the renovation works to the property, which adds value and increases the sale price. The property is then sold to a third party.

If you sell it for £145,000, you then give the owner the agreed £90,000 and you keep the rest. It will save you having to actually purchase the property and the acquisition costs around that. You will need to pay for the refurb and all works. You could even offer the owner an extra split of the uplift to make it really interesting for them. The vendor ends up making more money than if they had sold it in its original condition.

Cash: A question we always get asked is, should you find the money or the deal first. The answer is easy – both! You aren't going to find both at exactly the same time, but you will need both to be able to flip, so start looking for both now. Get educated so that you have the right knowledge. You will know your area better than anyone else because you have followed the steps from earlier on. You are the expert, you know exactly how to flip property, you make a great JV partner and people are looking to work with you. Tell them about the properties you are viewing, give details of the numbers and tell everyone what you do. You don't have to ask for money from people you just need to let people know what you do and how you can help people make a great return on their cash, and the money will come to you.

If you are at the beginning of your property journey we know for sure that you will read this and not believe us, because it's all new to you. You're probably thinking, '*Why would someone want to loan me their money*?' The answer to this is that you can create a win-win situation with minimal risk. There is risk in everything but property is easy to explain to people. They can have security as already explained, and you can offer them a fixed return on their cash. That is the simplest way to structure the deal.

When you are at work, with family members, out networking or even on the train, does everyone around you know what you do? Ok, that may be weird on the train, especially if you are on the tube as no one seems to talk to each other there. But at work, in the gym and the local pub and definitely with family members; people need to know as you never know who has a few thousand sitting in their bank account making very little interest.

Where to find potential investors and business partners

One of the pitfalls of being entrepreneurial is that you can sometimes become a bit like a magpie, drawn to new shiny things, chopping and changing before you've achieved anything.

I'm confident that you could think of a name right now of someone you know who flits about between different things, telling everyone they're really busy when you know deep down they're just chasing their tail and actually doing nothing of any significance.

You need to avoid being seen like this at all costs. It's tempting when you're starting out to try and be all things to all people, but you really do need to apply the Pareto principle to everything you do and realise that 20% of the invested input is responsible for 80% of the results obtained.

The fact that you're reading this book is a great indicator that you want to actually do something. Flipping takes time. It will take up 6–12 months of your life to do one property. It can be massively rewarding when you do this, but if you're the sort of person that likes to be seen doing a lot and flitting from one thing to another, then you're probably best deal sourcing for someone or a company that wants to get stuck in.

Still here? Great. The decision to Flip It! is one of the best decisions you can make because of the rewards it brings and the longevity of the relationship that you can make will set you up for life and enable to you build a sustainable business where the people around you stick with you and help you to build it.

As flipping takes a few months, it helps you to focus on attracting people who want to be in your life for at least a year. A year is the shortest JV contract that we typically do and because we make this clear, we attract people and investors who are more level headed, calmer about their investment and know that they don't need to pester us every 5 minutes to check their money is still where they deposited it.

Equally, because flipping is a systemised business, you will find that once you've established which builders, plasterers, carpenters, maintenance people, plumbers and electricians you get on best with, you know that you don't need to keep going out there to find new tradespeople to work with like you might if you solely focussed on buying single-lets all over the country.

Reactive services such as plumbers and electricians, who are typically only called by landlords in an emergency, are tamer if you also give them regular work on flips.

This has the knock-on effect that, provided you focus on one geographical area, you can strike up real relationships with people who will do those emergency call outs at a decent price and straight away when you phone them, because they've become part of your power team. I really can't emphasise enough the benefits that flipping can bring to the rest of your portfolio if you have one or are intent on building one.

Let's look at the different people you could joint venture with and the hats you might wear and when.

Friends and family: If you have already started out in property, do your family members really know what you do and how you can help them? Our first investors were family members. We started investing in property in 2006 and were using traditional bank lending to be able to purchase.

We would put in the deposit money and borrow the rest of the money from a bank. We paid the bank a percentage return (usually 5%–6% interest) and then sell the property, pay the bank back the capital sum and then go again.

Without using other people's money, you only have a certain amount of deposits yourself, or maybe none at all. No matter how much cash you start with, you will need to borrow money at some stage.

Our relatives had some cash sitting in the bank; it could have even been the same bank that we were borrowing from, so it was probably their money. Think about that for a moment!

In that scenario, we borrow money from the bank at around 5% interest per year, our family member has the same amount of money in the same bank and the bank pays them 1% (for example). Who was winning there? Yes, it's the bank! They lend people money for a higher amount, and pay the people saving money a much lower amount, taking the middle profit. They charge fees on top of that to both the borrower and the saver. The bank is definitely winning.

All we needed to do was take out the middle man/woman.

The shortcut is that we now borrow the cash from the saver. We pay them 5% which is what we would have paid the bank anyway, the saver gets the full 5% return, which is 5 times the amount than from the bank. They get the security they want from us, plus a great return on their money.

The other great thing is that once you have finished the deal, your investor doesn't really want the money back as the interest that the bank pays is so low, so they have a problem and invariably send the cash straight back to you for the next deal. You can then finance more deals and everyone wins.

Property meetings: There are many property meetings in the UK, just search the web for the phrase 'property meet' and you will discover some near you. Go there, turn up every month and get to know the people. JVs can come in the form of cash, they could be experience and they could even be the tradespeople you are looking for.

Your mortgage broker, solicitor, accountant, estate agent and JV partners can be found in these kinds of places. Get out there, tell people what you do and see who you can work with.

Property meets are great places for judging people and the services they provide by gaining social proof and speaking to others who have used them.

Don't rely on the yellow pages or property forums to judge who is most appropriate for you. As the saying goes: *'Confident as it may sound, a braying donkey in a field does not a thoroughbred make.'*

This is a business where you need to work with lots of people and you can't do this by yourself. It would be a very lonely slow business that way.

The aim with property networking is to be remembered as an expert in one particular area as quickly as possible. Therefore, you need to work on your elevator pitch. It might go something like this:

"Hi, I'm Karen and I'm a property investor from Cambridgeshire. I've been buying, renovating and selling properties in Cambs/Northants for the last 12 years with my partner, Tasha. We specialise in what has now become known as 'Flipping' properties, although we have a personal portfolio of single lets and multi-lets too. I buy houses with our money and money from investors too, so if you know of anyone who has any property deals, then we pay a referral fee for those houses that we end up buying. Also, if you know anyone looking to invest with an established company, let me know and if anything comes of it then we offer a referral commission too. We only work with a handful of people and only one investor per property because for us, this is a people business, so we only work with people that qualify and are great to work with. If I can help you in any way, just ask – we have lots of experience in the different areas of property investing and have a mentoring programme if you're looking to learn from seasoned experts."

Business groups: These are a bit different from property groups as you get a much wider spread of businesses here. Lots of the people who go to these groups are business owners. They may not be interested in property at all, however they may well be interested in working with you.

It's possible their business or they themselves have some cash in the bank, getting a very low rate of return. If you tell them how you can pay a much greater return, they may well be interested.

With business groups, it takes time for people to get to know you.

Don't go in on day one shouting about how great you are and how you can spend their cash; you need to be a little subtler, but it won't take long for people to get to know you. Be patient and the investors will come.

Business networking is very different to property networking. The chances are, when you join the right business networking group you'll be the only 'property' person in the group which makes you an instant expert and the other business owners there will respect that and see you as someone who has made sound investments in bricks and mortar.

There will inevitably be some people in the group who think that buying and selling houses is easy and anyone can do it; probably because they've moved to a new house in their life and made money in doing so, but you just have to rise above it and bide your time.

The business owners that you are really interested in, from an investment perspective, are the Independent Financial Advisors, Solicitors, companies with 10+ employees and franchise owners. These are the types of business where you are either trying to establish your credibility so that they will consider investing with you, or make introductions to their friends and family, who inevitably have cash to invest.

The other types of people you are trying to attract are the 'deal makers'. You know, the kind of people that want to make a quick quid from information. People in sales positions are great for this.

You should focus on telling them about the referral fee they'll get if they find you a piece of land, find you a property, or let you know about a friend or relative struggling to sell their property due to its condition.

Let them know you'll pay them £500–£1000 for any 'off-market properties' they bring you that you end up buying and you'll have their attention forever.

Inevitably you'll get the opportunity to introduce yourself to the room at a business networking meeting and you should take these opportunities whenever you can.

Here's an example elevator pitch for a business networking meeting:

"*Hi, I'm Karen and I own a property business. One side of our business focusses on buying, developing and selling houses. The other side looks after our portfolio of shared houses for young professionals – you know – like a student house but a million times better. I don't mind telling you, but we're up there with the most expensive rooms in the county and that's for a very good reason. We provide the best houses in the best locations and put the tenant's needs first. This means that our tenants stay for years and it gives our investors certainty that they'll get a great return on their investment. If you know of anyone looking for a hands-free investment that pays them 5% return on their money every year for doing absolutely nothing, then let me know and we can see if they're a fit with our company. We offer complete discretion, so if you're not the kind of person who wants the whole world knowing you've had a windfall, inherited some cash or you're just British and don't like to talk about money in front of people, then instead of chatting to me in the break, just email me and we'll meet up for a coffee.*"

There are many different types of business and property networking meetings around the country, and you might need to try a few before you find one that's the right fit for you.

You can usually attend as a guest for free for a couple of sessions while you decide which group(s) you want to commit to building relationships with. A Google search will quickly give you a list of relevant meetings in your area.

Mother/Father/Carer & baby groups: Obviously, this isn't for everyone, but if you are a new parent/carer and are going to these groups, then having a chat about your property business will certainly be a change from the baby talk.

Motivational speaker events: These events are great and usually over long days where you can really get to know people around you. The people at these events are always happy to talk and usually very motivated. You can make some great friends at these events and they can become JV partners.

Sports clubs: Playing sport is a very social event. Even in sports where you compete alone, you are more than likely participating in a communal club or at a venue where other people meet up afterwards for drinks.

Participating in sports demonstrates that you care about your health and have a commitment to something. Joint venture partners like this.

We met our PA at a sports club and it was easy to spot that she had the qualities we were looking for and conducted herself in a manner that fits with our company ethos.

We have also received investment from another member of the club and can only presume that they were vetting us as much as we were vetting them.

If you are looking for bigger deals, then you should think about activities such as golf or flying. That's not to say that you can't secure £100k from a football, rugby, badminton or hockey club. But the density of investors is likely to be higher where the activity that is being undertaken costs more than average or requires more time input to participate, even at the lowest level.

Pubs / wine bars (upmarket ones): People go to these places to relax and will often be more open and willing to talk about themselves and what they do. You will be able to see if there is any connection between you both in anyway, and if you could work together.

The gym, health clubs and fitness bootcamps: The healthcare charity Nuffield Health found that people who earn larger incomes were likely to go to the gym more than those gym members on low incomes. The study of 1,600 participants found that people on less than £20,000 a year went to the gym for an hour a week, whilst those with the bigger incomes went to the gym on average for 3 hours per week.

The same is likely to apply to bootcamps and health clubs where the membership costs more than your average Zumba class. Signing up to a continuous programme, maybe an 8-week course, means both you and they are more motivated to make a sustainable change to your health, and whilst bonding with other people who are on the same path you are more likely to meet people to work with. 12% of gym sign ups happen in January, but if you need to make some changes to your level of activity, don't wait, do it now. Joint Venture partners are there waiting for you.

Another study also found that 10.5% of the 2000 participants live with someone that they met at the gym, so if you are looking for more than a business partner, maybe going to the gym is more productive than writing and rewriting an online dating profile!

At work: Whether you love your job and want to stay there forever, or if you hate it and want to sack your boss, make sure you let people know what is happening in your life.

If you do want to sack your boss and you are building a property portfolio in the background, using flips to fund them, or putting that

£20k–£40k into a bank account from flips in order to pay yourself (as a cushion) when you quit, you need to tell them.

When I quit work, lots of people asked, "Where are you going", "Do you have another job to go to" etc. They often find it hard to understand that no, you don't have another job and you aren't looking for one.

Just let them know you will be a property investor and over time they will see you don't have to get up every day to go and work for someone else, you have the choice to create your own wealth and also help people along the way.

It's amazing, even years later when old friends approach you, interested in what you are doing, they may even have some money to invest with you, so help them get a great return.

On the train, bus or plane: If you like to travel, or regularly use public transport to get around, you'll know that there are some people who just like to plug in to their devices, and switch off from any social interaction around them. There are also those people who can't switch off, and like to have a chat with new folks around them. Be one of those people.

Take the opportunity to meet others, talk to them about what you do, because you never know who you may end up sat next to, or what situation they may be in. They may just be the one who has a property for sale, you never know!

On holiday: Sometimes you go on holiday and for the whole time you are there you see the same people or seem to be on the same dinner schedule.

This is the perfect opportunity to start a conversation, because being on holiday is when people really relax. Most people work all year to have that 2-week family holiday in the sun.

They let their guard down and will talk openly about their lives and what is important to them. If you are looking to fund a deal, you might just come across someone looking for a change of career or some extra work.

We met a guy while we were on holiday and a simple, non-contrived conversation has resulted in a potential joint venture.

These opportunities are everywhere and if you go into every situation looking to help people, you will be rewarded.

Facebook, LinkedIn, Twitter and Instagram: The golden rule – if you want to be seen as a legitimate business owner, stop sharing posts about weird pop bands from your youth and start posting about what *you* are actually doing in your life.

There is no need to overdo it, a few posts a week is enough and remember to include LinkedIn articles you have written and evidence of the contribution you are making to the world.

Also, stop sending Candy Crush or Farmville invitations and stop sharing questionnaires to find out what kind of flower you are most like. Stop poking people. This is not communication, it's just irritating!

If you have nothing to say, don't interrupt people who appear to be online with that little green dot next to their name. They are not waiting for you to poke them.

If you want to interact with someone, have a little think about what exchange of value you are giving. You are more likely to get what you want if you offer something in return. Karen recently had an exchange that went like this:

First message: "Hello Karen, Thank you" (presumably a thank you for accepting his friend request – in my mind this doesn't need an answer – it's not a question)

Two days later: "Hi Kay-Kay…hope you are doing fine today" (N.B. Someone's name is integral to their identity, so don't mess with their profile name. This will not give you your desired outcome. Even though there is a question there, it's not going to get a response because it's just spammy)

Half an hour later: "Sad you aren't texting me back... hope I didn't get things wrong".

My response: unfriended.

The bottom line is just because you can gain access into people's lives through having tens, hundreds or thousands of mutual friends, it doesn't give you consent to interrupt them just for your own gain.

The elegant way, when you get your first deal, is to post photos about progress and regular updates with pictures. Post about the exciting places you go, the meetings you have and the contacts you have made.

Make it fresh and exciting. Images are great as people haven't got time to read lots of words on Facebook. A great image and a few words will get much more interest and make people stop scrolling and start paying attention.

A great exercise to do is to look at your Facebook profile, Twitter profile or Insta through the eyes of someone who has only just met you or is about to meet you. That person will more than likely check you out on Facebook to see who you are and what you do.

So what does your Facebook profile say about you? How do you come across to someone new? You can delete old posts, or just hide them from your timeline.

A semi-naked picture from a stag do 4 years ago will be found if someone scrolls for long enough, and trust me they do (not me on a stag do, just to be clear) so make sure your history tells the tale you want people to see.

Also join appropriate Facebook property groups and contribute to them, be helpful and become the expert.

Your own website: When working with new people, most will Google your name to see what comes up. You want to make sure that it gives the right impression of you.

If you have a common name, then having your own website that ranks well will help people to specifically find you and determine if you are someone they want to work with. Having a brand to go alongside your personal name helps people to find you, and you should have both on your business card.

What is your online presence like? Do you have a website? What does that look like? Is it about you? Is it mostly about your company? What is your brand? What is your message? How do you want people to see you?

These are questions you need to think about and develop from the outset. You can only really be known for one thing alone, so pick your brand wisely and be proud of it.

The Buying Process

Once you have made the offer and had it accepted, it's vital that you get that deal through as soon as possible.

Unfortunately, in England, Wales and Northern Ireland you can still be gazumped. This means that right up until the day you exchange contracts, which happens after you have paid out for solicitors, legal searches and applied for bank lending; another buyer can come along and the vendor can accept their offer instead.

In Scotland there is a different system. Before a property can be marketed, vendors have to put together a home report which must include a RICS (Royal Institute of Chartered Surveyors) survey, an Energy Performance Certificate (EPC), and a completed property information questionnaire. You must instruct a solicitor to make the offer, negotiate on your behalf and check the contracts on the property. You'll need lending in place before an offer can legally be made.

If you are buying in England, Wales or Northern Ireland through an estate agent, they shouldn't keep marketing the property once you have had an offer accepted unless it is a corporate sale.

However, the estate agent wants the sale to proceed as they only get paid when it sells. Make sure you have the best solicitor in place to be able to achieve this quickly.

Your solicitor will work with the vendor's solicitor and also the mortgage lender. Unfortunately, you can't pick the solicitor used by the vendor and this may be the biggest delay when purchasing a property.

They often seem to be working to a different timescale to you and while that may seem like an unfair statement, remember there are no incentives for them to proceed quickly with the sale.

Vendors often slow down the process too by delaying sending paperwork back but don't let this put you off. Dealing with vendors is just part of the business and technological advancements will force improvements to occur soon enough.

There has been talk over the years of professional bodies developing an internet-based conveyancing system where you can track the process of a sale or purchase.

There was a failed attempt by Land Registry. Next it was the turn of The Law Society with their Veyo portal, which was to be marketed as '*the home of conveyancing*', allowing solicitors and licensed conveyancers to share information and documents with purchasers,

HM Land Registry and, eventually, HM Revenue & Customs, mortgage lenders and estate agents.

However, this portal was discontinued after commercial case management providers decided to create their own cloud-based systems as add-ons for products that conveyancing firms already use.

It won't be long before vendors and purchasers will be kept in the loop more efficiently through blockchain technology.

A benefit of buying a flip is that it is less likely that you will have to deal with a chain. A chain is when the person you are buying from is moving to another property and the owner of that property is moving to another property. Chains can be very long. In a chain everyone needs to complete their purchase at the same time so that everyone has somewhere to live and the lending on the previous property is cleared. Being in long chains can be a nightmare and you may well have experienced this when purchasing your own residential property.

For flips, when the property is generally empty or is sold 'with no onward chain', these are the best ones. Out of all of the flips we have done there was only one which had someone living there who needed to move out.

It was an interesting one, because the man who lived there was in some financial difficulties and we managed to avert the repossession.

He had lost his job and owed quite a lot of money on his property and all of the associated bills. We agreed to purchase the property to make sure all of his debts were paid off and he ended up with £30,000 surplus from the sale so that he could move on with his life.

The issue that presented itself was he was going to go into rented accommodation whilst he sorted himself out. As he had no provable income, the letting agent wanted him to pay for the whole 12 months' rent up front. He knew he would have sufficient cash from the sale of the property to do this, but he wouldn't get that cash until we completed on the purchase of the property, which left us with a problem.

Thanks to having a great solicitor, we agreed that upon exchange of contracts we would transfer him enough cash to be able to secure the rented property and move in prior to completion. We did this, and on exchange transferred £5,000 to him through the solicitors with a 2-week delay on completion to allow him to get the rented property and move in, which would leave the property we were buying vacant.

The slightly scary thing for us was that after he got the cash, he disappeared off to the Caribbean for a week. It was all fine in the end and he returned to complete the sale as planned.

The important point of this story is to make sure you have a good solicitor. To find one, ask other property investors who they use or would recommend and what kind of deals do they do. Do not stick with one if it isn't working for you.

There are plenty of great practitioners out there so quickly move onto one who specialises in what you need.

Your solicitor will need to carry out searches and write to you with any issues that arise from those searches. These can be things like uncertainty in what you are actually buying or land registry plans with dubious areas marked out.

They will check who actually owns the property, and make sure the person selling it to you is legally allowed to. They deal with the lender and will put a legal charge against the property on their behalf.

You will need to send them your deposit when requested, plus any fees and expenses. Your solicitor should be transparent with their fees and you should know from the beginning what you need to pay.

So when does an agent legally have to keep marketing a property until exchange of contracts? Well, it's with a corporate sale which is the politically correct name for a property that has been repossessed by the lender.

When you purchase one of these properties, the estate agent has to be seen to get the best price, and so they keep it available on the market until the exchange of contracts has been done. People are encouraged online through the property listing advert to make a higher offer than you.

In fact, the offer you make, which may have been accepted by the vendor will be displayed online for the world to see and advertised in the local paper. It will say, '*We are in receipt of an offer of £96,000 subject to contract for this property. Anyone wishing to place a higher offer must do so before legal exchange of contracts'*.

If you are in the process of purchasing a repossession to flip, having a good solicitor and broker is vital to ensuring you don't lose the deal to another buyer.

Trading property - 'the correct way'

This book is not designed to tell you how you should conduct your business affairs, nor do we give you financial advice. Your accountant will advise you regarding what information you must return to HMRC about the activities you are carrying out. To help you initiate those conversations with your accountant, we have included some information in the next section regarding Badges of Trade which HMRC use to determine whether you are trading or not.

The basis of the concept: A report in 1955 by the Royal Commission on the Taxation of Profits and Income reviewed case law and identified six badges of trade. HM Revenue & Customs (HMRC) has since reviewed further case law and now lists nine badges of trade:

1. Profit seeking motive
2. The number of transactions
3. The nature of the asset
4. Existence of similar trading transactions or interests
5. Changes to the asset
6. The way the sale was carried out
7. The source of finance

8. Interval of time between purchase and sale
9. Method of acquisition

Profit seeking motive: It is clear that having an intention to make a profit can indicate a trading activity, however by itself it is not enough.

In the case Salt v Chamberlain [1979], a research consultant made a loss on the Stock Exchange after trying to forecast the market. The loss was made after several years and over 200 transactions. This was not seen as trade and capital in nature. It was concluded that share trading by a private individual can never have the badges of trade pinned to them. These transactions are subject to capital gains tax.

The number of transactions: If you do something once, never to be repeated again, it is unlikely but not impossible, that you would be treated as carrying on a trade. If you keep doing it, it is more likely to be considered that you are trading.

The most notable case example of this was Pickford v Quirke [1979], where a syndicate purchased a cotton mill with the intention of using it in a trade, however, upon purchase they realised it was in a worse state than first anticipated. The syndicate then decided to strip the mill of its assets and sell it piecemeal, making a profit. They then repeated this a number of times with different mills. Due to the repeated nature of the transactions, it was determined that the profits were trading profits and taxable as such.

The nature of the asset: This principle looks at the asset; however, problems arise when assets are bought either as:

- An investment that has the ability to generate income
- Personal assets
- Some assets used by a trade such as plant and machinery.

An important case in this area was Marson v Morton [1986], where land was purchased by an individual with the intention to hold it as an investment. No income was generated by the land, however, it did have planning permission. The land was then sold. As the transaction was different to the taxpayer's normal activity as a potato merchant and was similar to an investment, it was not a trading profit. The transaction was not an adventure in the nature of a trade.

Existence of similar trading transactions or interests: This is best demonstrated in the case CIR v Fraser [1942]. In this case the taxpayer was a woodcutter who bought a consignment of whisky in bond. He then sold the whisky through an agent at a profit. Within the decision the judge stated:

> '*The purchaser of a large quantity of a commodity like whisky, greatly in excess of what could be used by himself, his family and friends, a commodity which yields no pride of possession, which cannot be turned to account except by a process of realisation, I can scarcely consider to be other than an adventurer in a transaction in the nature of a trade... Most important of all, the actual dealings of the respondent with the whisky were exactly of the kind that take place in ordinary trade*'.

Changes to the asset: It is important to take note of any changes or modifications made to an asset that may make it more marketable. In the case Cape Brandy Syndicate v CIR [1921], members of a wine syndicate purchased brandy from South Africa. Some was sent to the East with the remainder being sent to London to be blended with French brandy, re-casketed and sold at a profit. The syndicate tried to argue that the transaction was of a capital nature from the sale of an investment. It was held that a trade or business was carried on and was assessable as a trading profit.

The way the sale was carried out: HMRC states in its guidance that it is always a pointer if a transaction follows that of a 'undisputed trade'. The case CIR v Livingston and Others [1927], involved three unconnected individuals that together bought a cargo vessel. The vessel was converted into a steam-drifter and sold for a profit. The purchase was the first vessel the three individuals bought. An assessment was raised on the profit which was upheld as a trading profit. Within the decision the judge stated:

> '*I think the test, which must be used to determine whether a venture such as we are now considering is, or is not, in the nature of 'trade', is whether the operations involved in it are of the same kind, and carried on in the same way, as those which are characteristic of ordinary trading in the line of business in which the venture was made.*'

The source of finance: Determining the source of finance is important when deciding whether a trade is carried on. Finance taken out to purchase an asset, in the first instance, may indicate that to repay the debt the asset would have to be sold.

This was demonstrated in Lynch v Edmondson [1998], which concerned a self-employed bricklayer, who built two flats on a plot of land. Bank borrowings financed the property construction on terms whereby the loan would be repaid out of the sale proceeds from the first flat, a factor indicating that a trade was being carried on.

Interval of time between purchase and sale: The length of time an asset is held is an important indicator of trade. The longer the period of ownership, the greater the chance of it being seen as an investment rather than a trade. HMRC also look at the intention; if you can demonstrate an intention it could indicate the tax treatment.

In the case of Johnston v Heath [1970], the taxpayer was shown to have contracted to sell the asset before he had acquired it, and not surprisingly this was held to be an indicator that the intention was to trade.

Method of acquisition: Finally, it is important to look at how an asset is acquired. If it is inherited or gifted, it is a good indication that a trade is not being carried out, although this is not always the case. An asset acquired at a market or auction could indicate that it has either been purchased for a trade or an investment.

The case of Taylor v Good [1974], involved a taxpayer who purchased a house with the intention of using it as a family home. The taxpayer's partner did not approve of the house and refused to move in, which forced the taxpayer to sell the house immediately. The purchaser genuinely had the intention of not buying the property for a profit motive. As the sale was a short period of time after purchase it was still not deemed to be a trade. Within the decision the judge stated:

> '*Even if the house was purchased with no thought of trading, I do not see why an intention to trade could not be formed later. What is bought or otherwise acquired (for example, under a will) with no thought of trading cannot thereby acquire an immunity so that, however filled with the desire and intention of trading the owner may later become, it can never be said that any transaction by him with the property constitutes trading. For the taxpayer, a non-trading inception may be a valuable asset: but it is no palladium. The proposition that an initial intention not to trade may be displaced by a subsequent intention, in the course of the ownership of the property in question, is, I think, sufficiently established...*'

The likelihood is that at some point in your flipping journey you will be trading. However, if you are not flipping frequently enough, then it could be deemed that you should instead be reporting a capital gain. We can't give you the answer because we don't know your personal circumstances, nor are we qualified to advise you. The only way to be sure that you are reporting correctly to HMRC is to get advice from a suitably qualified professional.

Section 5: How to project manage with confidence

Section 5: How to project manage with confidence

Finding and managing people

Property is a people business. To have more success, you need to find the right people to perform the right roles. In this next section we detail who you should start looking for to enable your business to start or grow.

Cash is king. Deals, especially through agents need to be fast. If you can purchase with cash, then that is always the best strategy. However, don't think, '*Oh well, I don't have any cash*'. It doesn't matter to the estate agent whose cash it is.

The economy is always changing. We started investing together in 2006. We experienced the peak of 2007 and the following crash. To be honest, in the early days we didn't really notice the crash. Because we were doing this on our own and doing everything ourselves we were so 'in' the business we weren't aware of what was really going on. This was actually a good thing because we weren't listening to all of the negative hype in the media.

As James Caan says, *"Observe the masses and do the opposite"*. We were doing exactly this but without realising (or observing).

It was a static market for years, with the Bank of England Base Rate at 0.5% for 7 years and then the drop to 0.25%. Even now with base rate at 0.5%, there are many people out there with cash and a problem.

The returns they are getting in the bank are small, in fact with fees and inflation their cash may even be depreciating. You can help these people out by finding a great deal, borrowing their money and paying them a great return.

It's all about creating win-win situations as I said before. This really is a people business.

Broker: You will need to have a great broker who has access to the whole market of financial products. DO NOT use Buy-to-Let mortgages for flips.

When you offer on a property through an estate agent they will offer you the use of their mortgage advisor. These people can be great for the residential and buy-to-let mainstream products, however you will often be looking for a more commercial product.

You can make a real business from flipping so you need to do things right from the start by using the appropriate product. Use cash (yours or someone else's), bridging finance, commercial finance or a development loan. Get a great broker who can advise you on what is available and get that lending through for you fast. Speed is key here.

Solicitor: You need a solicitor who is used to dealing with property 'deals', not just simple residential purchases. You don't want to be waiting three months to get the purchase through, you want to purchase fast. Time is money and your profit is at the end. If you hang about too long, you may miss out on some great deals. Make sure your solicitor is capable of getting the deal through fast.

Accountant: Your accountant should, in theory, be able to increase or improve the effectiveness of your business by more than the cost of their fees.

If you are new to property, then there will be things you don't know you can legitimately offset and ways to manage and plan your tax affairs that you simply won't have learnt at school or as an employee.

As you progress and become more experienced there will be other benefits of having a decent accountant, such as the potential to socialise with the other major clients they serve. Often accountancy firms will hold seminars, networking dinners and away days.

If you ever feel like you are schooling your broker, solicitor or accountant then it is time to change to a new firm.

Estate agents: These are your best friends. Build relationships with them from day one. When the market is low they will be knocking on your door. When the market is busy you need to make sure they know you are serious and can act fast. This takes time and dedication, but you will get some great deals this way. Treat them well. Go to viewings when you say you will, offer and stick to it and get it through fast. That is the formula for a great relationship. There may be many estate agents in your area. Start with the independent agents, as these usually have the smallest turnover of staff and you can get to know them. Do try the bigger chains and view anything which is in your flip area.

Tradespeople: You are going to need to get people to do the work, so you will need quite a few different tradespeople on board. Make sure you get at least three quotes for each job. In the beginning, you may go through quite a few trades, because until you actually start to use them you don't really know how it will go.

Once you get your main team, stick with them, pay them on time and make sure you are clear on what you want. If you change the goal posts, then do it early and be prepared to pay a bit extra.

Having the right team of people is crucial; they need to communicate and work together. They may come up with ideas you haven't thought of.

All the planning in the world is great, but sometimes, until you actually start to do the physical work, there may be things you missed in the original assessment. Be prepared to work with them. Make them tea or take them some coffee and cake when you visit the building site.

Neighbours: There are some jobs that might require permission or assistance from the neighbours and often a shared effort can cut the time of the task in half. A good example would be clearing ivy from the front of a house, especially if it has rooted itself in both properties in a terrace.

On one occasion we started removing the ivy and the neighbours who were Polish tenants came out to help and do theirs too. They had the biggest bin bags I have ever seen which came in very handy.

Although we had very few shared words, it was a great job to do together and we got by with smiles, hand gestures and a lot of pointing.

A highlight of the job was when a pair of lacy knickers fell out of a section of ivy just under one of their bedroom windows. I think it was either from the previous tenants, or maybe they just weren't phased by it because they hid their blushes well and none of the men owned up to them being theirs. Either way, they ended up being swung around on the end a broom handle for a while before making their way into the bin.

Planning and scheduling your works

Getting works done in the correct order and to a schedule is key to maximising your profit; so, let's explore what to do and when.

Pre-purchase preparatory work: The first thing to do, even before you get those keys on completion day, is to have a measured survey done of the property. You can do this yourself, usually on a second viewing and either double check the agents' details, or just use their floorplan outline and add your own dimensions.

Accuracy is key: When measuring a property, you can use a regular tape measure, we recommend getting an 8m one rather than the standard 3m ones. If you want to be a bit more flash, you could get a laser measure. We have one which was about £100 and worth every penny. Stick it on your Christmas list if you're one of those people who are tricky to buy for and get everyone to chip in. It'll save you going through another year of receiving brain teaser tricks with bits of interconnected hoops, or yet another toilet humour book.

You want to note down the exact dimensions of each room as you walk around the house and pay specific attention to the following:

- Location, condition and size of windows, especially the height from the floor in the kitchen to see if you can get a standard height worktop under it if reconfiguring.

- Location, condition and size of radiators. Are there any rooms without radiators?
- Location of plug sockets, noting whether they are singles/doubles. Are they in the correct position for the bed/sofa when you dress the property for sale? Are there enough?
- Location and condition of the boiler. Is it in the best room to maximise the space? If you need a new boiler and it is located in a bedroom, you might want to consider moving it to the loft, kitchen or housing it in a bespoke cupboard. If it's not being flued out of the roof you'll need it to go on an exterior facing wall for the flue, so bear this in mind before planning to move it.
- Location of any chimney breasts, recesses or built in cupboards.
- Location of the stairs – does the slant of the stairs ceiling come up into one of the bedrooms? If so you might want to think about making a built in bed over it to maximise the space left in the room.
- Location and condition of light fittings. Are they privacy lights i.e. nearer the window in the bedroom than the centre of the room? This can look quite dated and make rooms feel dark when it is easily relocated to the centre of the room.

- Location of the bathroom light – are they IP65 rated, or has someone just stuck a lightbulb in there? You may question whether people would do things like this, but in one of our flips we found that in order to switch the light on in the bathroom, you had to climb over the bath taps and into the bath to reach the light pull. The light connected was just a lamp holder which was completely non-compliant with building regulations.
- Location of the water stopcock. It is usually not economical to move the mains water feed into a house, so you need to know where it is and ensure that it remains accessible when you redesign the layout.

Video recording: It's great to keep a record of the property. The easiest way to do this is as soon as you open the front door. Just switch on your recording device and video the whole property. This is something we do every time. You can capture images from the video later to see great before, during and after shots.

Damp survey: Once you have decided on the location of the kitchen, bathroom and ensuite, it's time to get that damp survey done. This should be done before you purchase the property and can be instructed by the agent acting for the seller.

The damp and timber condition report is usually free of charge because the contractors want the work, and it can be a great bartering tool to bring down your purchase price if damp is found.

Quotes will vary by thousands of pounds so get three quotes. Most properties in the UK have a certain level of damp, some of which is acceptable, but it can be a deal breaker if it comes to the end of your refurb and you haven't addressed an underlying issue. If your surveyor discovers the property has damp, then so will your buyer.

If there is damp, which is quite likely in older properties, then you definitely want to deal with this as part of the strip out process as soon as you get the keys to the property.

The damp treatment company will need all of the plaster to be taken off the walls on the ground floor to a height of at least 1.2m. They will inject them with a resin and then re-plaster using a specific plaster mix. Get this organised fast upon completion of the purchase.

Meters and utilities: Locate the electric, gas and water meters and take readings. It's also a great idea to take photos so that you don't lose that scrap of paper you are writing on.

If you want to, or have to, change the utilities to the house, then you must start this process early as it can take a long time to organise; and we don't mean switching your electric supplier, we mean having to relocate or physically move them.

Gas: You may need to move or update the gas supply for a number of reasons. Perhaps the gas into the property where the gas meter is located is in the garage and you want to do a garage conversion and it would be in the way.

To be able to move this, you will need to contact the National Grid to organise connection. They will initially make an appointment to come out and have a look at what needs to be done, then let you know the cost of the work.

If you agree to the quote, they will then schedule a date to do the work. This can be many weeks or months away, so make sure you action this straightaway away when you get the property.

The property may not even have a gas supply to it. You first need to see if there is gas in the street. You can do this by contacting the National Grid, or you can simply look at the other properties to see if they have a white box on the outside wall with a gas meter in it. If the street has gas, then you can have it too and you should.

It's surprising how many properties now have mains gas in the street, but not all of the homeowners have upgraded their properties to make use of it. It is quite commonplace with older people who have managed without having a gas meter for their whole lives.

Resolving this and getting a gas connection is fundamental though as the generation of homebuyers that we are targeting will always have had gas in their homes and may be put off if it's not available.

The opposite of this is true in some villages. If there is now a gas supply but they have been used to oil, then people may stay with oil because of the investment they have made in having an oil heated system and the low price of kerosene (at the time of writing). This may change in the future, but don't be put off buying a property to flip in a village that doesn't have mains gas.

You can still improve the finish of the property by upgrading the old rusty oil tank for a double bunded plastic one, or better still, get it sunk into the ground so that thieves can't pinch the oil by sticking a tap or a heated piece of copper pipe in the side to form a readymade spout.

To get a gas connection you will need to contact National Grid and organise a site visit, get a quotc and agree to the work before they will schedule it in. The price of this varies depending on where the gas is. If you are down a country lane, then it's probably not economical to run a new gas main for a half mile and they probably won't do it. If the supply is in the footpath directly outside the property, then it's a much easier job than if it's in the middle of a main road.

If the gas main is located in the middle of a busy road, then they may need to organise groundworks and traffic lights if they need to dig the road. You will bear the cost of the extra service too, although they will organise this.

Sometimes there are schemes which discount the price of a new gas supply providing that it's not a new build or a conversion. If you don't qualify for free connection, then there may be alternative discounts available. These are often linked to the areas classed as being in the top 25% of deprivation, or occupiers being in fuel poverty based on income.

To check the availability of discounts and offers, head over to the National Grid website and you will find up to date information there.

If requesting a new gas supply to your property, you will need to organise to dig the ditch to accommodate the gas pipe across your land and to the gas meter box.

Your Gas Safe Engineer will be able to connect the house supply once the National Grid engineer has fitted the meter.

Electricity: It's rare that you need a new electric supply into a flip property, unless you need to move it during works such as a garage conversion. You will often need to upgrade the consumer unit (also known as the fuse board), but your electrician can do that easily.

If the supply before the consumer unit (the tails) need to be changed, then the UK Power Networks would have to do this. It can be expensive to move the incoming supply to a property; at least £738 for overhead cables, and £1,026 to relocate an underground supply.

These minimum prices include the cost to supply a new meter box, but alterations can take 6–8 weeks from payment, so avoid it if you can, unless the alterations make it financially viable.

There will be additional costs if they need to dig up the road, get highways approval, council approval or incur parking costs, plus there might be third party costs from a builder and electrician.

Water: If the water pipe coming into your property is made of lead, there may be a scheme in your area to receive a free lead-replacement service.

Check this out with the local water authority to see if they offer this service. If this is the case, just give them a call and say you would like a lead replacement installation and they will organise it all for you.

Again, you will need to organise someone to dig the part on your property and lay the blue MDPE pipe at the depth as instructed by your water supplier. There will be a minimum and maximum depth. Your plumber will connect this into the new meter supplied (usually at the end of the drive) and into the property. Doing this will give you choice as to where the supply can come into the property and also a new, working, stopcock for the property.

Find out how to turn the water off: Each house should have an internal stopcock to enable you to turn the water off from coming into the house, however in old houses (the ones you are buying to flip), these can be very old and may not turn or may not work.

You will need to find out how to turn the water off outside the property. If updated then there should be a stop tap outside the property under a round plastic plate, usually with '*water*' embossed on the top. Under that you may find polystyrene black cover which you lift out to reveal the off tap. At one of our flips we had to turn off the external stopcock as the internal one had seized.

We located the main stopcock, opened that up and removed the polystyrene only to find a giant nest of ants! Karen got the job of putting her arm through the ants' nest to turn off the water. Just at this point a man two doors down the street came running out shouting, "*You can't turn that off, we all have our washing machines running, you are turning off the water to the street*", and then proceeded to knock on everyone's doors telling tales.

Now, it can often be the case that the stopcock will turn off multiple properties. In this instance it wasn't the whole street, it was just our property.

He also had the cheek to tell us that that he was a landscape gardener and if we wanted the garden done he would be happy to quote. Needless to say, he didn't get a chance to quote, let alone do the work.
Property is a relationship business and he hadn't made a good first impression.

You need to make sure you know which houses each stopcock isolates before turning these off so that you don't upset the neighbours from the start. You can tell if each house has one because there will be a circular access cover about the size of a side plate that says water on it outside each house. If there isn't one on the footbath on the perimeter of the property, whatever you find may serve many houses. The neighbours will usually know if they have lived there for some time, so just ask. Once you have isolated the property, you can get the plumber to change the internal stopcock so that you don't have this issue again.

Sometimes, you've just got to get on with it though. Many years ago we bought a property and on inspection discovered that there was no internal stopcock in the property for the mains water supply and the one for the street needed a T handle which no one had to hand. This is far from ideal when doing a refurb because at certain points, such as removing the kitchen, bathroom or boiler you need to turn off the water supply.

Trades such as plasterers need access to water so you can't just cut it off permanently. Also, you really want to keep a flushing loo and a sink with running water for cleaning brushes, washing out buckets, and making tea or pot noodles. The only solution was to create our own stopcock.

We protected the rest of the house with golf umbrellas and drew straws about who was going to be the lucky person (Karen) that got a sustained cold power shower while they did the deed and replaced the stopcock. That was a make or break decision because once you've started, you have to keep going until you've finished the job.

You'll never quite appreciate how much pressure 'mains pressure' water is until you have to remove a section of pipe and try to get a new stopcock in the pipe run. It is definitely the right thing to do though, as it means you can control the water to a project without turning the whole street's supply off every day.

Keeping the neighbours on side is a major priority for us and we have found that they play an important role in your power team.

They are great for local knowledge, knowing tradesmen, finding out the history of a property and making toast and a good cuppa!

At one house we made friends with a neighbour when Karen overheard her reading the instructions for setting a new rotary washing line into the garden. Karen heard the instructions being read out by her to her teenage son; "one-part cement, two parts water, three parts sand, that's fine, we have water so we'll go for the two parts water option".

Obviously, it was Karen's duty to save this poor lady from the swamp she was about to create and ask if she needed any help. With the straightest face she could muster, she said she had heard the instructions she was reading out and suggested that it was a mix for concrete and that she needed all components, not just one as it wasn't a one or the other choice.

Planning your works : Once you have a measured plan of the property, you can properly start to plan the works that will add value. Start with the kitchen and bathroom – are they in the right place? If not, move them. Does the master bedroom have an ensuite? If not, could you fit one in? Adding one could probably add £5,000 to the value of the property in the right location whilst costing you just £1,500 to install. It should also get you a faster sale than a house without one.

Order of works: Your initial viewing and assessment will have given you the basic idea of what you can do with the property. You will have already worked out the best use of space and how you can re-configure it for maximum resale value whilst sticking within budget.

Once you have the keys to the property you can really start to plan the refurb. On the initial viewing you never really get to see everything, however thorough you think you have been.

When you buy from the same estate agents all of the time they'll probably let you sign the keys out once you've had offer accepted and before exchange of contracts (if it's an empty property). Some will want to accompany you though, so don't be offended if you don't get this special treatment straight away.

So now you need to get in there and really plan the project. Allow a few hours to do this properly. If you get this done right the first time, it will save you lots of time in the future.

Measure all of the rooms and spaces and write them on the floor plans. You should already be picturing and planning how are you going to add value before you complete on the purchase.

Is it a garage conversion, layout change, adding an ensuite, moving the kitchen, moving the bathroom?

You should always take a few copies of the current and proposed floorplans to site. This is to ensure you have ALL of the details

Here is an example of a floor plan taken from one of our projects.

We often use the estate agent's original plan and then alter it to create our own basic template of the works we want to do.

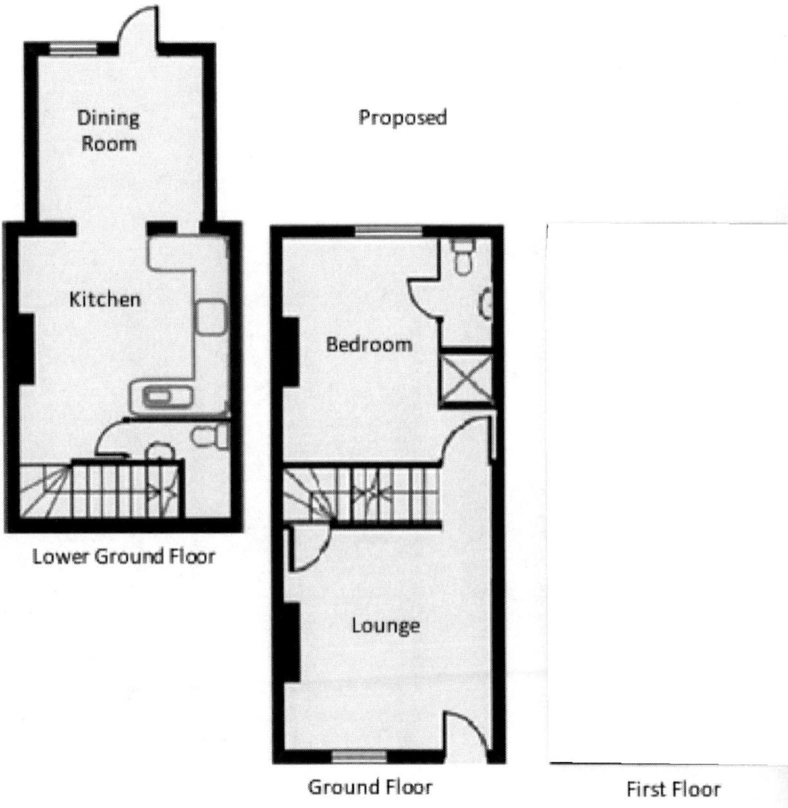

Once you have the new walls/rooms in the right place, next create a key for the floorplan, maybe a square with a cross in it for the light switches, a rectangle with two lines for a double socket and a thin rectangle for the radiator.

You want to be able to interpret this later on, so make sure you understand your symbols and abbreviations.

Mark on the floorplan where the following are:

- Radiators
- Sockets
- Lights
- Consumer unit
- Water main inlet (stopcock)
- Gas meter (if mains gas)

If you are replacing windows and/or doors, it's a good idea the measure these at this point and add the dimensions to the floorplan.

Also measure each room. The original floorplan from the agent may or may not be correct. If you have done it yourself then you know it's right.

Always measure the size of the windows and note the condition; these measurements will be really useful later in the project when you need to order curtain poles, curtains or blinds.

You'll be able to refer to your original floorplan and order online with no need to revisit the property time and time again to re-measure everything.

Proposed floorplan changes: These floorplans are your blueprint from the start. Spending half a day on this at the start of the project will make it run much smoother and avoid any doubt with the different tradespeople you use. The key to a successful refurb is communication - written as well as verbal.

Plumber's floorplan: Next you want to start to plan and draw the new layout. Mark where the bathroom sanitaryware is going, and where the is kitchen going. Where do you want the radiators, appliances and sockets? Do you need to add any new radiators?

When working with your trades, it's really important to be clear and for both of you to understand what is needed. It's all very well meeting up on site and having a chat, but if nothing is written down then the interpretation of what's required may be different.

That's just human nature, so have a floorplan for the plumber. Mark on it where the water supply coming into the property is, where the existing boiler / water tank is, and where all of the radiators are located. Then create a summary of what is being replaced and what is needed new.

If you are going to buy radiators, make a note of all of the sizes and get them ordered and delivered to site as soon as possible. If you can be flexible with time and when you need jobs done, then a plumber can quite often work around that.

They may have a cancellation in a couple of days and if they know you are flexible and you get jobs done quicker, they'll give you a call and say can they start tomorrow. If you're ready with the materials, then the answer can always be 'yes'. Getting the project moving quicker is always a bonus.

The floorplan you give to the plumber shows them where you want anything new. For example, if they are moving the boiler, you'll indicate this on the floor plan. If you are adding an ensuite, you need to indicate where you need the hot and cold supplies to run into the room. The same goes for the kitchen. Where are the washing machine, sink and dishwasher going? Are you having an American-style fridge-freezer, and does it need its own water supply? These are the things you need to identify from the start.

Electrician's floorplan: On the floorplan, or 'schematic' for the electrician, you want to mark the location of consumer unit and whether it being replaced or not.

It's unlikely that the location of the consumer unit will change during a refurb unless you are converting an office with three phase supply into a house.

Even if you are doing a garage conversion, you would usually be ok with the consumer unit being in there after completion of the works because it'll be a habitable room, just as most other locations in the house would be.

You should mark clearly where you want any new sockets, extractor fans and lighting and don't forget outside lighting here too. In the kitchen you will need an extractor. If you are changing the use of the room and it wasn't previously a kitchen, then building control will want the extractor to vent to the outside of the property.

You will need to plan out where the oven and hob are going so that the right cabling can be run to these locations. Sometimes a single oven will just require a plug, but most other types of cooker including ranges and double ovens for example, will require a separate feed, plus a supply for an electric hob and the cooker hood.

It's best to get in as many double sockets as will be required from the outset. Corners are a great place to put two double sockets, above the worktop level, but make sure that there are no sockets too close to the oven or sink. Your electrician will advise what the regulations are at each refurb you do as this will change over time and unless you are an electrician you won't be qualified to make those decisions alone.

Don't forget to include under-counter sockets for appliances such as washing machines, dishwashers and tumble dryers. Also, it is handy to know that at the time of writing, the regulations for gas and electrics are two separate things. Just because your electrician is happy to sign off their work near a cooker, it doesn't mean that when the plumber comes to connect the gas hob that they will install it if there is a socket right behind it.

Remember, as your project progresses, and things get added, the qualified tradespeople will only sign off what's there at the time they sign it off.

Before purchase, but assuming you are proceeding: Below are the key points to consider when assessing the costs associated with your refurb:

1. Due diligence – is the property Listed/Article 4 /TPOs/Conservation Area/Requiring specialist surveys?
2. Measure the property properly
3. Plan the works – kitchen, bathroom, new openings, driveway
4. Quotes for damp/timber treatment

5. Quotes for skips/grab lorries (you'll need at least one 8-yard skip if you are having damp treatment and/or removing any brickwork). Cost should be £170–£250inc.
6. Builders quotes for any structural work– get three quotes
7. Electrician quote for a re-wire – get three quotes
8. Plumbing quote for a new system/boiler – get three quotes
9. Quote for new windows/doors – get three quotes
10. Quote for decorating
11. Contact approved contractor for drop kerb/driveways
12. Ask the availability of contractors
13. Set up auction site searches for furniture to dress the property

Planning access: Something else to consider with each property is whether you are intending to put a drop kerb or new driveway in. If you are, then you might want to think about removing any hedges along the front perimeter of the property that are going to be for the chop, so that you can pull an extra vehicle up off the road.

You must check before you do this that there is nothing preventing you from doing so, like it being a protected hedge or a property with an Article 4 direction.

We like to remove hedges straight away so that we can get a skip in the front garden instead of on the road. This will keep the neighbours happier for longer because it means they can all still park in front of their houses and there's no obstruction on the path or road.

It also deters 'skip rats' (a term of endearment for people who rummage through your skips looking for bits of timber to burn in their log burners), especially if you leave a lamp on in the property on a timer overnight.

There's no complete way to stop this kind of behaviour, but if you keep a tidy site and the neighbours on side, then you will be afforded a bit more goodwill by them, which is especially important when a delivery arrives on site before your trades and the neighbour's door gets knocked on at 7am by the courier with your parcel.

Materials: If you are ordering materials, then start to put together a list of the items you will purchase. Once you have done your first flip, lots of the materials will be the same. The quantities may differ, but most houses will need the same materials. You should create your own spreadsheet detailing the following:

- Date
- Supplier
- Materials/Items
- Quantity
- Price

The spreadsheet should be updated with each project to keep your eye on the market trends and the times of year to buy certain items.

For example, if you are using a trade kitchen or bathroom, some suppliers will have discount at particular times of the year. Keeping an eye on this, especially with companies that have a retail side of their shop, will help to reduce costs which ultimately means more profit in your pocket.

Keeping the project on track: You will need to create a schedule of works. For many people this can be really daunting. Don't worry though as we have a version for you to start with. Every project will vary, but the main parts are the same, and once you have this you can re-use it, adding to it for all of your future projects. Quite often the hardest part is the first time. Then it just gets easier and easier because you know what you need to do.

The first project will be a little bit of an unknown with the actual timescales, as everything is new to you. Do put timescales into the plan but be prepared to switch or alter them as you go. Do this for the entire project and you will have a great starting document for the next one which matches your natural rhythm and management style.

You will be able to see where you can get things done in a more efficient way. Again, be rigid in keeping this up to date and you will have a document that will save you time and money for the next project.

If you use *www.estimators-online.com* to work out your material and labour costs, then their report will also include a project plan and schedule of works for you to work from. Alternatively, if you want to create your own you can go to: *www.tashaandkaren.com/fi-resources* to download a schedule of works template to complete.

Once you have a date for completion of the purchase: You usually get the keys to a property on a Friday, regardless of how many times you tell the vendor's solicitor you can complete on any day of the week. In advance of this you want the following lined up for the following week:

1. Instruct a Building Services company to do the calculations for any structural works you are having done, such as removing walls or ask your builder to get their structural advisor to start.
2. Submit your Building Notice (this is explained in the next section) detailing what works you are doing. If your Local Authority has a good reputation, then use them to sign off the Building Control aspect of your works. If you think that there may be an issue with speed of service or they're not the best,

then you can use a private Building Control company to sign off the works.

3. Notify the Local Authority of your intention to start the works detailed in your Building Notice. Ask them to do a site visit to discuss the planned works. You need to give 48 hours' notice, but they might come out the next day in some regions.

Paying the tradespeople: You pay for works only when they are complete. You could agree a JCT contract (see this website for more information – www.jctltd.co.uk) to formalise how the project will progress. However, you could also consider doing a less formal, but well documented, agreement with staged payments during the refurb. It depends how complex the project is. Trades will have subcontractors to pay and materials to buy.

A good builder should be able to put together a schedule of their works. Then at each stage they will be able to tell you that certain parts are complete and you can pay for that section.

If you are organising them all, it is down to you to go and check to make sure everything you have agreed with them is complete. If you have a site manager or lead builder, then they will be able to do that and have an online version which you can access to see how progress is going.

Don't pay the final bill until everything (including all of the snagging) is done.

Once the main build is done and there are only small bits left, a tradesperson may have a few big jobs lined up for other people and your little bits may not be important to them. They will do them but may pop in as and when they can between other projects. This is no good to you because you need everything done to be able to market and sell the property. Get it all done and then pay the final bill quickly.

Regulations: One of the things you must do is keep on the right side of every council department, government body, strategic authority and regulatory body when it comes to flipping property. Don't ever be tempted to take short cuts.

People's safety, the quality of the finish and the speed of sale will come down to one key thing. Have you done everything correctly?

When it comes to getting sign-off by Building Control and/or the Planners, they will need to see that any change of use, extensions, and general changes to the property have been done correctly. There are horror stories of people bypassing the right avenues and trying to shortcut the system. Don't be one of them - it's a false economy.

Additionally, if you are offered a property and it looks like a part-finished project, then it would be foolish to take on that property without fully inspecting it with an experienced builder to see what they have meddled with.

We recently viewed a property advertised as a 'part-finished project just requiring its finishing touches'.

We were checking out the agent just as much as we were the property to see if they were the wheeler dealer type, and they were.

The property had a half-finished loft conversion that never would have passed Building Control as none of the timbers were tied into the walls, and even if they had been, they weren't the right gauge to support a ceiling, let alone a floor. Additionally, there wasn't enough head height at the top of the very wobbly set of stairs (which looked like they had been bought from eBay with a child's a tree house in mind) to pass building regulations. Needless to say we didn't buy it!

Just be careful if you come across these types of projects. Sometimes if, unlike the previous example, what has already been started has been done correctly, they can be quite economical to finish, but they are priced accordingly and you might overpay in the first instance which breaks rule number 1 (buy for true market value or less).

So where do you start when thinking about which departments would be interested in your development? Well its simple. The council have two interested departments:

1. Building Control
2. Planning

Building Control: Building regulations are minimum standards for design, construction and alterations to virtually every building. The regulations are developed by the UK government and approved by Parliament.

The Building Regulations 2010 cover the construction and extension of buildings and these regulations are supported by Approved Documents. Approved Documents set out detailed practical guidance on compliance with the regulations.

You can apply to your local authority building control department or Approved Inspector for building regulations approval. For more information, visit *https://www.planningportal.co.uk/info/200128/building_control*.

An application will either be done through a Full Plans application or Building Notice. The council will have a fee schedule which determines how much you pay depending on the number of things they need to check and the number of visits.

That fee does not go to the particular building inspector that comes out to your property, it goes into the council coffers to be split amongst all of its statutory services, of which Building Control is one. There is no point feeling like or acting like 'you own them', because you won't get the best out of them.

We all want the properties we sell on to be safe, so if you assume from the outset that Building Control can help you to achieve this, you'll be setting out on the right footing and are more likely to have a harmonious relationship with your council.

Planning: To find out if your project will need planning permission, contact your Local Planning Authority (LPA) or a qualified planning consultant. You'll probably need planning permission if you want to:

- Build something new
- Make a major change to your building, e.g. building an extension
- Change the use of your building.

There are also some non-council bodies that might have a statutory interest in your project, depending on certain things about the property and its geographical location. The main authorities would be English Heritage and the National Parks Planning Authority.

They all have different roles. If you want more information about the standard of works that should be undertaken, then a great resource is www.*planningportal.gov.uk*. Your local council might be a great source of information and it's really important to find the right department and approach them in the right way. In a former life I worked in local government and I can honestly say that the vast majority of people working there weren't 'jobsworths' as some people say.

They genuinely wanted to get things done efficiently (and by the rules). It's key to remember that the person who comes out to inspect the work you are doing didn't make the rules. He or she is working within a set of guidelines and they literally do not want to be revisiting your site time and time again to make your life difficult.

Certain areas of the country are protected because of their natural setting or because they have historical significance. You may come across Listed Buildings when viewing flips and if it is your first flip then you may not want to over-complicate things by buying a Listed Building. That said, if you like a challenge, they are rewarding projects to do.

There are three types of listed building: Grade I; Grade II* and Grade II.

The vast majority of properties that you will come across for sale as a home will be Grade II. Exactly the same checks and balances by Building Control will be applicable, but as well as planning permission, you will need Listed Building Consent for any alterations and sometimes repairs where the material fabric of the building is affected.

This is still just a process that you either do correctly or fall short of.

In our experience, working with Conservation Officers can be straightforward, provided that you are doing simple things to the property. If we are looking to purchase a Listed Building, we will email the council and ask their opinion of the works we intend to do and ask if there would be anything that might affect the likelihood of getting permission.

The basic upgrades that you do to a flip property will normally be plain sailing, provided that you stay on the right side of the Conservation Officer. These are people who have specialised in this area and spent many years studying and honing their craft. They usually have immovable opinions about what an area requires which is grounded in passion for old buildings and a dislike for people who try to spoil them.

So with that in mind, please respect special buildings and the people who work to protect them and you will have an easier passage.

Sometimes a Grade II or II* property might be in the vicinity of a Grade I property, such as a church, and so the Conservation Officer would have to consider the group value of both properties and as such might not permit an extension to the Grade II, as it would affect the setting of the Grade I building. We wouldn't expect you to know this, and for the most part you will probably stick to run of the mill brick houses that all look the same and are nowhere near anything of historical significance, however there is quite a nice niche there if you are particularly interested in heritage and bringing older building back into use.

Once you have the keys: This is the general order that you will schedule works to happen in:

1. Conduct a general inspection of the property to make sure nothing needs your immediate attention. Check the electric meter for debt as well as you will need power in the property
2. Get a skip delivered
3. List any items of value such as stair lifts, outbuildings, greenhouses, furniture etc. that are surplus to requirements on eBay, and get the buyer to come and remove them. Note, the part of a stair lift that has the most value is the seat part, especially if it is one that has a remote control. There are mobility companies that will come and remove the whole stair lift and take it away if the seat is decent
4. Instruct removal of any loose items that are not staying, such as carpets, laminate flooring, vinyl, lampshades, blinds, curtains and any furniture left behind by the vendor

5. Instruct removal of fixtures and fitting such as the tiles, flooring, sanitary ware (try and keep a useable toilet for as long as possible to keep trades happy, otherwise you might find them using the garden. If it is a large project, then your main contractor will manage the site and the legal requirement to have a welfare unit and portable loo.
6. Get the strip-out team to remove any items that you have agreed to do outside of the damp treatment contract. This could include removing any skirting boards, kitchen units and plaster on the ground floor up to 1.2m in height
7. Clear the garden and keep on top of mowing the lawn
8. Get the chimney swept
9. Order new kitchen if there is a lead time. Get as many 1000mm units in as possible as this reduces the cost
10. Instruct a decorator to start prep work. Strip all wallpaper that isn't staying. If it is an older property and there is a chance that using an electrical steamer will blow the plaster underneath, advise them to then use a spray bottle like the one you'd use for spraying house plants and scraper. If labouring yourself, remember to apply the Pareto principle and spend 80% of your time spraying / soaking and 20% scraping. Abraham Lincoln said, "*If I had six hours to chop down a tree I'd spend the first four sharpening the axe*". The same applies to stripping wallpaper

11. Get damp treated. Remember to notify neighbours if required under the Party Wall Act
12. Order the materials/tools such as acrow props, lintels, insulation, timber, plasterboard required to do any structural works if you are project managing the site, or get your builder to start the works detailed in the Building Notice
13. Order new sanitary ware (toilets, baths, basins, shower enclosure, shower tray)
14. Build ensuite structure and all other new partitioning
15. First fix plumbing, electrics and drainage
16. Plaster boarding
17. Plastering
18. Second fix plumbing, electrics and drainage
19. Fit ensuite and new bathroom suite
20. Tiling the bathroom(s) and ensuite(s)
21. Fit internal doors
22. Get quote from carpet fitter
23. Order paint and laminate flooring
24. Installation of new windows/doors
25. Decorating – ceilings in white and walls in grey or white, kitchen and bathroom in appropriate paint
26. Fit kitchen cabinets, work tops and tiles
27. Fit kitchen flooring – retain some old carpet to put by the back door for wet/dirty shoes

28. Notify Building Control of completion
29. Build decking, weed treat any pathways and driveways
30. Paint exterior of property if it is rendered
31. Order soft furnishings
32. Get carpets fitted
33. Get windows cleaned
34. Furnish the property, including bedding and curtains
35. Dress the kitchen for dinner
36. Buy some nice flowers
37. Get estate agents' valuations
38. Instruct an estate agent
39. Get electrical/gas certificates
40. Get FENSA certificate
41. Have a glass of wine!

Selling the final product: Do you dress the property to sell it? 100% YES without question. You are creating a home for people, so you should use fairly neutral colours to appeal to the mass market. You need to add the homely effect through the furnishings.
Let's walk you through the property.

As you approach the property in the car, you are happy to see somewhere to park off road, and a really well-maintained front garden. It looks easy to look after. The front of the property looks maintained, the windows and doors are all white uPVC and look brand new. The render on the property has been painted very recently in white. The guttering is black and again looks good as new.

You open the nice new uPVC front door and step onto a quality door mat with plenty of space to remove muddy boots if needed. It's a bright but chilly evening, and as you step in the property you feel the warmth of the house, the heating must be on, it feels really homely.

You notice the carpet is soft and neutral in colour, the stairs are ahead of you and there is a bright teal lamp shade on the centre light. You turn right into the lounge where the walls are white, and the gloss on the woodwork is bright white. There is a nice 'chic-shadow' grey feature fireplace wall, with a modern chrome fire on the chimney breast.

There are two comfy looking leather sofas with scatter cushions and a coffee table in the middle. There's a window at each end of the room with nice bright curtains and matching lamp shades for the two ceiling lights. There is also an obvious space for a television in the corner of the room, although there isn't one there. There are some really nice paintings of bright flowers on the wall above the two sofas. At the far end of the room are bright white patio doors leading to a very tidy looking garden.

Next you walk into the dining room with a long glass table and matching dark brown leather chairs. You see a table runner along the whole length on the table and a nice green plant on the table in a copper coloured pot. There is a window to the front with some classy curtains and matching lamp shade in the centre of the ceiling.

As you walk into the kitchen you notice the natural daylight flooding into the room from the two large windows. There is also an external door to the garden. There are clean white vertical blinds in the windows.

The brand-new kitchen in oak style shaker with dark black worktops and wooden oak style flooring looks good, as does the silver oven with a five-ring hob oven and a matching silver extractor hood above.

Everything looks so clean and new. You are imagining living in this property and how you and your family would use the space. There's a stainless-steel Franke sink with a black washing-up bowl and a lemon tea towel hanging on the hook at the end of the cupboards. A stainless-steel kettle and toaster are on the worktop.

You can see there is space for a large fridge freezer at the end of the run and you think you may even be able to fit a round table at the far end under the window for breakfast.

There is space for a washing machine and dishwasher, which is a relief because you just hate washing up.

You go into the downstairs bathroom; it has a new bright white three-piece suite. The bath has a shower over it with a nice shiny glass screen. The window has a teal roller blind and there is a towel to match on the chrome towel rail by the sink. There are some bright coloured bath bubble and shampoo bottles on the end of the bath. The flooring is smart black tiles.

You head upstairs, as it is probably best to do the garden last. As you walk up the soft stair carpet, the light floods from a window in the hallway above. There are 3 bedrooms in the property; a single room to the right with a single bed perfectly made up with a nice white duvet, grey throw, matching scatter cushions, curtains and lamp shade. There is a nice wooden bedside table next to the bed and plenty of space for a chest of drawers.

The second bedroom is larger and has a double bed, perfectly made with 2 bedside tables each with a matching lamp, there is a nice large canvas above the bed, the colours contrast with the curtains and main lamp shade. There is a built-in wardrobe with hanging space and lots of room for more storage.

Now into the main master bedroom. It’s a little bigger than the last one and similar in décor, but this has another door which leads into an ensuite shower room which is bright and airy. You see a chrome finished sliding quadrant door shower in the corner with a bright white WC and sink. Duck egg coloured roller blinds hang over the two small frosted windows and there's a matching towel on the chrome towel rail. The wooden flooring and a chrome threshold look great.

Walking back onto the landing, you notice another door. Inside there is a cloak room with WC and basin, and a chrome towel ring and wooden flooring, perfect for a family home.

You go down the stairs, back through the kitchen to the back garden with freshly cut lawn and decking outside of the patio doors. There is also a wooden picnic table with the sun shining on it.

At the bottom of the garden is a decent sized wooden shed to store all of the garden tools you have collected over the years. There are a few really well-kept pots of shrubs. Sounds like a dream, right?

If you have chosen the right location, appealed to the right buyer, been realistic with the resale price and done an amazing job of the refurb, then you have set yourself up for success.

The 6-month rule:

We're often asked how long it takes to do a flip and people seem surprised when you say 6 months. But that is the reality when you take into account the works and time it takes to push a sale through to completion once it's on the market.

The vast majority of people who buy our flips are doing so because they are family homes that they want to move into themselves and so they purchase it with a regular residential mortgage from the high street.

Some high street banks and building societies want the vendor to have owned the property for at least 6 months, otherwise they consider it to be a sub-sale and it makes them twitchy.

The date that they go by is the date that your solicitor registers your purchase with land registry, so you want to make sure that they expedite that process as much as possible.

It is sometimes possible to get a mortgage through before the 6-month rule has been satisfied, however we are going for mass market appeal in order to get the best possible price for the property, so we start to market the house at around 4 months with the intention of finding a buyer and getting the process completed as close to 6 months as possible.

We do this by letting the estate agent know when the 6 months are up so that they can inform any potential buyer and see off any conflict from the mortgage providers.

It is possible to sell a flip quicker than 6 months. There are two ways of doing this; the first one being if you can find a cash buyer. Cash buyers obviously have no mortgage lending and there is no restriction on the amount of time someone has to own a property before it transacts to another owner.

The second way is to sell at auction. Auction properties, however, tend to have issues so if you are selling a shiny refurbed property at auction you may not get the best price for it as people there are looking for a bargain or a property to add value to themselves. They will also be viewed with suspicion and won't attract your regular type of buyer.

Getting your paperwork in order: When you are flipping property and you have gone through the process of finding, negotiating, planning, buying, using all of the systems we have explained from R.E.S.E.A.R.C.H. to P.A.W.S., you finally get the finished product. We find that the most exciting part.

In fact, Karen always says the most exciting time is the night before the carpets go in. She knows that when that time comes, everything is finished. Well, almost. You just need to furnish the property. You have gone through the whole process; the estate agent is keen and ready to market it for you. You have a queue of people ready to view.

You sell the property quickly and want to get it through as soon as possible, as your payday is at the end and only at the end. Everyone else has been paid along the way, you are the last, but because you have done a great job it will be worth the wait.

The offer is in and you want to push things through fast to get your cash. You can make sure that you have the best solicitors and estate agents that understand that you want to get it through fast.

However, if you haven't got all of the paperwork sorted out, you may end up being the one who delays the completion. That may even cause the chain to break in the buying process. So make sure you have all of the documentation ready. So, what do we mean by documentation?

New boiler – Certificate and guarantee: If you have a new boiler installed, you will need the installation certificate from the plumber. The boiler will also come with a guarantee which your buyer's solicitor will ask for.

New Windows / Doors: If you have any replacement external windows and doors you will need a FENSA certificate which stands for Fenestration Self-Assessment Scheme. If you use a window company who are FENSA registered, they should automatically put this through and the certificate should be posted to the address within a few weeks of installation.

They aren't always very fast at doing this or may even forget. Most people who have windows replaced in their family home wouldn't ask for one, because they don't really need one.

You need one and the buyer's solicitor will ask to see it. So, once the windows are installed, ask them to get the FENSA certificate to you as soon as possible. Ask them how long it normally takes, make a note in your diary and ring them again if you don't have it by that date.

Electrics: If you have any electrical works done at the property (which is very likely in a flip) then you need the electrician to issue you with the appropriate certificate. They should do this at the end of their work, detailing exactly what they have completed.

Damp: Most old houses have some form of damp and you will need to resolve this to sell it on. If you get damp proofing done at the property through a proper damp proofing company, this will come with a guarantee. It can be anything from 10 to 25 years; just make sure the company have issued you with this once the work is complete. This should be available straight after the work is complete and needs to be transferable to the new owner of the property.

Building Control: If your builder has done any works requiring Building Control approval, then it will need to be signed off and a certificate of completion issued to you.

Summary : Make sure that each and every one of these documents are in your pack as you go along and chase them if they are late. If you do this efficiently, you will not have issues that hold up the sale in the end. Remember, if the sale is delayed, then you are losing money.

Ongoing costs whilst refurbishing and marketing the property

While you own the property you will be responsible for the following bills until completion of the sale:

Gas: Even if you aren't using the gas during the refurb (it is a good idea to turn this off from the start), then there is still a standing weekly charge which you will need to pay. Unfortunately, the gas supplier won't let you turn it off for zero cost.

Electricity: You will definitely need to leave electricity on as your tradespeople will be using it all of the time. Make sure you have the initial meter reading. There are different meters; Pay-as-you-go card meter, and a standard meter.

Some of the flips you buy will have a pay-as-you-go style meter in where you have to top-up a card to be able to get the electricity. This would have been installed to help former tenants or the owner to budget. Despite this, these meters can rack up quite a debt when the property has been left empty. You are NOT responsible for this debt when you purchase the property and the debt can be reset to zero. There is a process for this and it can take a few days, so get this done early.

When you get the property, check the meter for debt. Our biggest meter debt was £175. You just need to call the supplier. To find out which utility company currently supplies a property with gas or electric, you can call the Meter Number Helpline (0870 608 1524) and provide your gas meter number to find out who your gas supplier is.

To find out your electricity supplier, call the appropriate regional number listed on the uSwitch website (*www.uswitch.com*).Tell them how much debt is showing on the meter and they will send you a new card to reset the meter.

The card should arrive the next day and you just need to put it into the meter until it shows zero debt.

Once it has reset you can top-up at a local shop. If the meter isn't pay-as-you-go, then the easiest thing to do is setup a direct debit to pay a monthly amount. This way you don't have to think about it and won't get those red bills that come through the door.

Water: You will read the meter when you get the property and know the starting point. You will need water for the refurb, so will have some costs here. If it's a metered water supply, you will pay for just what you use, otherwise there will be a standard yearly cost which can be split down into monthly payments. The easiest thing is to setup a direct debit so you don't have to think about it again until it sells and you take the final reading.

Insurance: Make sure you have insurance. To help with cash flow, you can get insurance policies that you pay monthly, which can be more expensive, however these can sometimes allow you to finish them early and get a refund after 6 months. Or you can pay yearly for a lesser amount, although that means that you may not get as much back if you cancel it at sale.

Make sure you continue to insure the property whilst it's on the market. Insurance is one of those annoying necessities, because hopefully you will never need it, but it's essential when you do. Never try to save money by not insuring the property.

Council tax: Historically you could get the first 6 months free from council tax if the property was empty. This changed in most areas and may well change again. In most areas empty properties attract a council tax premium, so it is in your best interest to get the property finished quickly.

Go onto your local council website and find out for your area if there are any free empty home periods and how to qualify. If not, you just have to pay it. It is easier to set up a direct debit so you don't have to think about it again.

You will only pay for the time you have the property and if you overpay, they will always refund you. That's the same with the gas, electric, water and insurance.

How to get the sale

You need to make an impression on a potential buyer fast. They will make a decision about your property within a matter of minutes of getting to the viewing.

Kerb appeal and the street scene are important. What is it like when you first drive up to the property?

The initial look and feel as they enter the house is equally important. Get it right and you will get the sale. Remember, you are creating a product that people really want to buy. It's quite often an emotional decision to purchase a property. Make it amazing; somewhere people aspire to live, something they want to be proud of and somewhere they can take their friends.

Once all of your works are complete, ask a friend or colleague to come to the property and look at it through the eyes of a potential buyer. Make sure they haven't been before so that they have no idea what it was like for comparison.

If you are at the property quite a lot sometimes you don't see what others see. It may be something as simple as a crumpled curtain, or some paint work not quite cut in straight. Take on board their comments and improve where you can.

Should you go back to the estate agent who sold you the property? Well this depends. If you promised as part of the deal of you purchasing the property from them that you would go back to them then yes 100%, you should always keep your word in business.

If you have a preferred agent in your area to sell through, but you happened to purchase with another, there is nothing wrong with going to that one, as long as you didn't make that promise.

Don't forget you will be looking for a short lock-in term with the first agent to give them a chance to sell at a premium price. This needs to be a maximum of 8 weeks, 4 if you can get it. If it's a hot property at the right price in the right area, it will sell fast, so they should be ok with that. Once that fixed period is over you are free to go with other agents if you think that would help.

The initial agent should be prepared to keep your property on their books as they have already done all of preparatory the work for it and it doesn't cost them anything else (except viewing time) to keep it on.

We often hear, 'well it's on *rightmove.co.uk*, so it doesn't really matter which agent it's with as everyone just looks at *Rightmove* and whatever the agent they call them'.

There really is much more to it than that. Yes, most people will look online and see everything that is available and they won't be put off by which agent is selling it, however the way the agent communicates with both the potential buyer and seller is key to selling your property.

The way they show the buyer around the property is also key to the sale being achieved. Some agents will just turn up at the viewing and leave the potential buyer to wander around and then just leave with no questions and no follow-up call.

They believe that if the buyer is interested then they will call the office. Again, not true.

Interacting more with the buyer to find out what they really want and how that property can work for them will make a huge difference.

Who should do the viewing? We think it should always be the agent for a number of reasons. Firstly, if the owner of a property does viewings, the potential buyer will not feel relaxed. They won't feel that they can ask the same questions.

They may even feel rushed and not look at the property for as long as they would with an agent. Any questions they have that the agent can't answer should be fed back to you fast and answered quickly by the agent. If you have a good agent, then this shouldn't be an issue.

The only time you should agree to do the viewing is if someone is coming to the area at a time when the agent is closed and can't do the viewing. This would usually be evenings or weekends.

It's better to get the viewing than not at all and the buyer can always do a second viewing if needed with the agent at a later date.

If you do have to do the viewing, make sure you give the buyers time and space, don't bombard them with facts. Tell them you are happy to take questions, however you will leave them to view at their leisure and wait in one room or even outside for them.

Keeping the property marketable

Imagine the scene:

You have been flipping awesome and got the project through on time and on budget. This is exciting, you are about to go into selling phase. You have picked your estate agent and got a great term and rate, everything is sparkly new, and it has kerb appeal.

For most people this is the time to relax sit back and wait for the sale, which means payday, the day you collect your well-earned profit.

But wait, there are a few things you need to make sure you keep on top of and organise during the sale of the property.

It may be that on sale day when that board goes up and the first viewer goes in and everything is perfect, however there is still maintenance to do, especially in the summer months.

It's amazing how fast grass grows, and the weeds manage to grow even quicker. Organise a gardener to go over a least every fortnight to cut the grass and have a general tidy up, unless it's winter and not much grows.

In your own home I bet you get quite a few leaflets, newspapers and flyers through the door, but as you live there, they just get recycled on a daily basis. It's amazing how quickly these mount up when you leave a property. The door mat fills with junk mail in no time. It will very quickly get to the stage where it's even tricky to open the front door. The property may have been like that when you bought it. It wasn't the best impression, was it?

The best thing to do is ask your estate agent to inform you in advance of any viewings so that you or someone can go over and pick up the post and have a general check around the property.

Also, it's worthwhile making sure there are no spiders in the bath or dead flies on the windows sills. This only takes a few minutes to do but makes a massive difference. Sometimes, the estate agent will get a viewing which must happen on the same day. You don't want to be the one to lose a potential buyer, so it's worth popping over regularly to keep on top of these things, just in case you don't get enough notice to go over there before the viewing.

If you are on a pay-as-you-go meter, make sure that it is topped up. There is nothing worse than getting a viewing on a cold, winter's night and when they get there they are viewing by phone light as there is no electric. Needless to say, this will not get you an offer on your property.

In the winter, heat the house ready for viewings. Ice on the windows and being able to see your own breath will not make people want to buy your house. They need to feel as if it's their own property; warm and inviting. If you get enough notice of viewings, then get that heating on. Otherwise leave it on low to make sure you don't have any issues with ice and broken pipes throughout winter.

Accepting an offer

Keep calm! This is the moment you have been waiting for. You are now on the other side of the fence as you're normally the one offering on a property.

Now people are making offers on your property and it's an exciting time. This is why you are doing this, to sell the property, and you now have an offer. You should already know what you need to sell the property for to reach your required profit, however don't tell the agent this otherwise that is all they will aim for.

This part comes down to time *versus* cost. You want to be able to sell fast, otherwise you are racking up more bills every month. You will know from your workings out at the start of the project how much that property costs to maintain each month, including gas, electric, water, council tax, insurance, gardener and cost of finance.

Have this number in your head. Each month you are 'losing' this amount of money if you don't sell. Now with the numbers, when you worked out your profit you did your costs projection for 12 months.

Hopefully your first offer will come at 0 - 6 months. If you sell earlier than your working out period, you'll be even more happy with more cash in your pocket. The quicker it sells the more you make. Be realistic with the price and know your numbers.

Don't always accept the first offer, unless it's what you're expecting, especially if you have a number of viewings lined up. You can use the things in the property as bargaining tools and a way to get a little more cash.

In our first Flip we dressed the property as described earlier. It looked great, and we were really pleased with the finish. That property was aimed at a first-time buyer who by definition doesn't usually have much furniture to bring to the property. The buyer really wanted to include the furniture in the sale so we got an extra £3k on their original offer and didn't have to move the furniture out.

The furniture probably cost about half of that, so it puts extra cash in the bank. If someone walks through the door, offers the asking price and is a cash buyer with no chain, then you are definitely winning.

Your perfect buyer:

- Cash
- No chain
- The offer you want
- Wants to move fast
- Has fallen in love with your property

Pushing for a completion date

Once a price is agreed, make sure you know what the timescales for completion are. Your solicitor will send you a contract and a property information pack to fill in. You will need to fill in a section for each room in the property and you will need to list what is included and what isn't included in the sale.

Get this done quickly and accurately and get it back to them. When negotiating the sale, you may have agreed to leave curtains and certain furnishings. Make sure you list everything agreed in the document.

Then make sure you keep in contact with your solicitor and the selling estate agent for updates until your flip is SOLD!

The next step will then be to repeat the buy, renovate and sell process with your next property (and as many times as you like), ensuring that the due diligence you now know how to do is as good in your tenth year of business… and beyond.

Epilogue

The information and stories in this book are taken from our own personal experience of over a decade of property investment. The reason for us putting pen to paper is to inspire you to take action.

When we started, we didn't know anyone else who was doing this, we didn't know of any education, seminars or teachings we could go to so, we just went for it.

Today, there are experienced people (including us) teaching you how to invest in property and there is some quality education out there.

We would advocate getting educated, but most importantly taking action, and starting to make things happen. You'll be surprised at how quickly you can get this rollercoaster to wealth going.

We finally found other property investors and great mentors in 2011 and went through a massive change in our journey. We could see that it was going to be possible to both sack our previous bosses and live the life we wanted to. We could see the path to choice, freedom and getting our time back. We have loved our journey and still do today.

We continue to flip and invest in cash flowing assets, and we have no plans to stop as we love it so much. We have focussed on the parts of the business we're great at and have built teams around us to leverage out the rest.

This has given us time to do the things we love, like sourcing and negotiating deals, planning and designing the finished product, writing this book, delivering courses on buying and selling property and running our application-only mastermind groups.

Trading property isn't a get-rich-very-quick system, however if you are prepared to work smart for a while so that you don't have to forever, wouldn't that be worth taking action for?

We really hope that you have got value from this book and that you can see a way to change your life in whatever way you want to. One of the most rewarding things in life for us is to see people making a success of their own and their family's lives.

We look forward to maybe meeting you in the future and sharing our stories of success.

Here's to your wealth and happiness!